Local Financial Management
in chools

Ed by Peter Downes

Basil Black

Published by
Basil Blackwell Ltd
108 Cowley Road
Oxford OX4 1JF
England

British Library Cataloguing in Publication Data

Local financial management in schools.
1. Great Britain. Schools. Financial
management
I. Title
371.2'06'0941

ISBN 0-631-16085-X

ISBN 0-631-16086-8 (pb)

Typeset in 10.5 on 13pt Sabon
by MULTIPLEX techniques ltd, St Mary Cray, Kent.
Printed in Great Britain by T.J. Press Ltd, Cornwall

Contents

Preface   iv

**PART ONE: What is Local Financial Management?
How does it work in practice?**

A brief historical background   3
The aims and objectives of LFM   5
The scope of LFM   7
Distributing resources to schools   20
LFM in operation   23
LFM: responsibility and participation   30
Reservations about LFM   32

PART TWO: Personal perspectives on LFM

1   My hopes for LFM
     John Brackenbury   41
2   A councillor and governor's view
     Robert James   48
3   LFM in a primary school
     Audrey Stenner   60
4   LFM in a secondary school
     George Thomas   75
5   Implementing LFM across a whole LEA
     David Hill   98
6   A finance officer's perspective
     Haydn Howard   111
7   The impact of LFM on an LEA
     Tyrrell Burgess   130
8   Future perspectives
     Brian Knight   146

Conclusion   164
Bibliography   165
Notes on the contributors   169

Preface

This book has been written to meet the rapidly growing interest in Local Financial Management (LFM) as a way of organising the financing of schools and of improving management in schools. Interest in LFM has been increasing over a number of years through the well-tried process of innovation and pilot schemes. An added incentive for achieving an understanding of LFM comes from the probable inclusion of the delegation of finance in the 1988 Education Act.

It is important for readers to be quite clear about the purpose behind this book.

It is not:

- a political tract devoted to promoting an innovation which might be seen as a lever to achieve other changes of a politically more contentious nature. The contributors and I regret that LFM has become politicised to such an extent that people may become prejudiced against it because of their disapproval of other measures included in the Education Act.

- an academic treatise on the history of state school funding.

- an attempt to 'sell' a particular model of LFM. We regard as futile and irrelevant the claims and counter-claims being made as to the invention of LFM. It is clear that a number of initiatives have been taking place, quietly and within the relative obscurity of the world of educational administration, for 30 years or more. It is the particular conjuncture of educational and political change that has brought LFM into national prominence.

- a considered and comprehensive response to the July 1987 consultative document which goes considerably beyond LFM as such, eg in its proposals in connection with the appointment of teaching staff.

This book sets out instead to offer a practical guide for those who may well be faced, within the next few years if not at once, with setting up and administering LFM schemes, whether they want to or not. It seems to me essential that those of us who have had some experience of LFM should make it available in a concise and readable form so that others may take some short cuts in their preliminary work and avoid at least some of the pitfalls. This sharing of experience is particularly important at a time when all of us in the education world face innovation on an unprecedented scale. If we are not to be overwhelmed by the flood of new initiatives and developments, we must be prepared to share experience and expertise with each other.

That is why I was pleased to respond to the invitation to edit this book and have assembled a team of contributors who have something of value to share with a wider public. I am very grateful to them for working under considerable pressure of time to produce an LFM anthology which will, I believe, meet a widely-felt need and provide a useful reference-point, albeit in a rapidly-changing situation.

In *Part One*, I have tried to provide a fairly straightforward and factual account of how an LFM scheme works in practice. The example used is the Cambridgeshire model but this does not mean that it is being recommended uncritically as the only possible blueprint for LFM. If part of the essence of LFM is sensitivity to local needs, it is logical that schemes must bear the characteristic mark of the particular circumstances for which they are devised. The imposition of a single format of LFM from Cornwall to Tyneside would contradict its basic purpose, that of giving flexibility to meet locally-assessed needs.

I am very conscious that readers will come to this book with wide and varying experiences in school financial management. Much of what is included in Part One is basic and I beg the indulgence of those who find it to be a statement of the obvious. I am also aware that educational practice varies widely across the country and that everybody does not start on LFM from the same background; that is why Part One is necessary. I have included a chapter on the main reservations about LFM, although, given the Government's determination to introduce LFM, it might be argued that the time for objections has passed already. I would argue that reservations must be carefully noted if new schemes are to be devised which will command the wide respect and support of those they are supposed to be helping.

Part Two is the more important section of the book in that it explores various perspectives on LFM. Most of the contributors have been caught up in the Cambridgeshire scheme in some detail, and they examine the ways in which this has affected their professional role and their attitudes to education. Chapters 7 and 8 of Part Two have been written by experienced educationalists who examine the implications of LFM for the Local Education Authority system and for the longer term future.

It should be stressed that all the writers are giving their own personal view and are not writing an 'official' account, as they might to a Government department or County Council committee. Although they have been asked to look at LFM from a personal perspective, their contributions will to some extent overlap as it would be quite impossible to keep such a wide-ranging scheme in water-tight compartments. Sometimes their views differ and they may unwittingly contradict each other. This too is not surprising as each one has been invited to write individually without seeing what the others have written. This achieves a spontaneity of approach which will reinforce the point already made, that we are not trying to present a ready-made solution with all the snags ironed out. What the contributors *do* share is, on the whole, an enthusiasm for the experience of LFM as it has affected the schools they have worked in or the LEA system as they have experienced it.

Whatever format the future financing of schools takes, it is quite clear that Heads, Deputies, teachers, LEA staff and Governors are going to need training. We hope that this book may provide a useful starting-point for such training and, to make extension work more manageable, we have suggested discussion topics, role plays and seminar activities at various points in the book. Finally, we have provided a short annotated bibliography for those who would like to do further reading.

In addition to thanking the contributors to the book, I should also like to express my appreciation for the help I have received from my colleagues at Hinchingbrooke School, especially Sheila Hargreaves (Deputy Head i/c finance) and Clare Plumbley (Senior accounts assistant); from Tom Bowker, a colleague in the Secondary Heads' Association, and from my wife, Pamela Downes, who has brought an invaluable lay-person's mind to bear on the topic. The contribution of Tom Hinds, formerly Second Deputy Chief Education Officer in Cambridgeshire and now Director of Education in Hillingdon, deserves a special mention: he has kindly commented in detail on Part One of this book and, as lead-officer for LFM in Cambridgeshire from 1981 onwards, has played a major part in the development of the scheme.

Peter Downes

Part One:
What is Local Financial
Management?
How does it work in practice?

A brief historical background

As explained in the Preface, there is little point in attempting to construct an exhaustive catalogue of all the many schemes of 'local financial management' in existence and no value at all in attributing the creation of the concept to any individual or any area of the country. To a greater or lesser extent, Local Education Authorities have for many years been giving schools the freedom to spend a proportion of the money available to them in the way best suited to their own needs, *as perceived by them*. That, in its simplest form, is the essence of LFM: the transfer from the LEA to the individual establishments of the power to spend their allocated money.

As long ago as 1950, Hertfordshire introduced a 'cheque-book scheme', giving Heads their own general account, with responsibility for stationery, materials, textbooks, library books, repairs of furniture and equipment, purchase and replacement of smaller apparatus, cleaning materials, first aid materials, school visits and postage. Unspent balances could be carried forward but special authorisation was needed for items over £150 (primary) or £250 (secondary and special). All salaries and wages were excluded.

The Inner London Education Authority introduced a scheme called AUR (Alternative Use of Resources) in 1973. This gave schools an authorised minimum teaching and non-teaching establishment, plus capitation. An additional resources allocation was made which could be used at the discretion of the individual schools in buying in more staff, subject to a ceiling of 80% of the AUR allocation.

Other small scale schemes were attempted in the 1970s: R.T. Spooner, Head of Rodillian School, Leeds, writing in *Education* on 19 June, 1987, speaks of a project in Leeds which, he claims, produced a number of short-term advantages but soon withered away. Jim Hendy, Director of Education for Stockport, writing in the same journal on 2 October, 1987, refers to a 'low-key circular to schools in Somerset' around 1970 which gave them the facility of virement.

In 1981 a new generation of more far-reaching schemes began when **Solihull** set up a pilot scheme with three schools, extended by 1987 to 10 (a Sixth Form College, six comprehensives and three primaries). The significant step forward here was the inclusion of expenditure on teaching and non-teaching staff, as well as buildings and grounds maintenance. In the Solihull scheme, headteachers have freedom to spend money largely as they wish and can carry forward any under or over-spends from one financial year to the next. A plan to credit or charge interest on carry-forward sums is under consideration. Solihull's original intention was to produce a cost-saving scheme but it has cost money to run because of the centralised accounting procedures. The pilot scheme has been well received by administrators and teachers.

Cambridgeshire introduced a scheme of Increased Financial Responsibility (IFR) in 1977, giving schools the responsibility for the certifying and coding of accounts and, more importantly, for the budgetary control of capitation and other minor items of expenditure during the year. This helped pave the way for a more ambitious pilot scheme for LFM which was introduced in April 1982 for eight volunteer schools (six secondary and two primary – one primary dropped out after three months). The scheme was not introduced as a cost-cutting exercise but 'to enable the Governors and Head of each school to make the most effective use of the resources available to them and to give each Head flexibility within an agreed budget to manage the school.' The scope of the scheme was not dissimilar to Solihull's except that building and grounds maintenance were excluded. The introduction was hasty (and much criticised for that) but after an initial year (1982–83), in which a number of teething problems were sorted out, it became more effectively operational from the following year. Its success was such that by 1987 it had been extended to all 46 secondary schools and a further pilot scheme for 10 primary schools (selected this time not as volunteers but to produce a representative sample, including some heads with strong reservations), was set up for a three year period (1986–1989).

In 1976 the **Cheshire** Authority started a scheme which progessed district by district until all 82 secondary schools were involved as 'limited cost-centres' by 1984–85. The items included in the scheme were: furniture and fittings; textbooks; library books; stationery and materials; administrative, educational and domestic equipment/ supplies; printing, office stationery, postage and telephones; educational visits, staff travelling and subsistence expenses; income; limited virement over salaries of staff who leave during the summer term. Fuel was added subsequently.

By 1987, pilot schemes, or limited cost-centre schemes, were in operation in over 20 Local Education Authorities. Even without the added impetus of the Government's proposed legislation for the 1988 Education Act, the LFM bandwaggon was firmly on the road.

From this brief survey, a number of major issues arise which will be addressed in a concise and factual manner in Part 1 of this book and dealt with more discursively, from a variety of perspectives, in Part 2:

- What is the basic purpose of LFM?
- What should be included in such a scheme and what excluded from it?
- How does it affect administrative procedures within the school and the LEA?
- What benefits have been gained and what problems encountered?
- How have the roles of head, governors and teachers been affected?
- How can consultation be made to work?

Part 1 concludes with a chapter on the main reservations which have been expressed about LFM, but without further comment or discussion at this stage.

The aims and objectives of LFM

There is no copyright on a concept such as LFM. It is merely an evolving idea with multiple applications and interpretations. Hence there is no formal summary of what its aims and objectives are. The following is a composite, based upon a number of schemes and experiences. It suggests two global aims, with a number of more specific objectives.

A OVERALL AIMS

i To enable the governors and head of each school to make the most effective use of the resources available to them.

ii To give each head flexibility within an agreed budget to manage the school.

(Cambridgeshire, 1982)

B OBJECTIVES

1 **To give schools a sense of autonomy and institutional pride**

   a Governors, heads and staff will have a greater sense of responsibility and an enhanced self-image when an LEA demonstrates its confidence in them by delegating financial responsibility.

   b Efficiency, economy and job-satisfaction are promoted if decisions are taken by those whom the decisions most directly affect.

2   To extend the scope of management within schools

a By giving the power to individual schools to move money from one heading to another, those at all levels in management begin to see more clearly the inter-relatedness of the component parts. The effect can be to enhance teamwork and increase mutual awareness and appreciation.

b By enabling human time to be costed in financial terms, it is possible to find more cost-effective and equally satisfactory ways of running a school. (*For example, how many heads and deputies spend a great deal of time on low-level administrative tasks which could be more cheaply (and more effectively!) accomplished by a member of the ancillary staff on less than half their salary.*)

3   To improve the flexibility and speed of management

a The streamlining of administrative procedures by giving heads executive power within an agreed contingency budget can reduce considerably the day-to-day crises which contribute so much to tension within schools.

b The concept of LFM recognises that, although all schools are involved in the common task of education, they are all slightly different and have particular needs and individual solutions which cannot be recognised or legislated for by the LEA, however sensitive its officers are, because of the fact that they are at some distance from the problem.

4   To increase understanding of educational issues and to stimulate participation

a LFM is a means by which Governors are brought to a detailed examination of the needs of their schools and are stimulated to find ways of meeting those needs.

b It is our educational responsibility to make sure that the costs of education, which is funded out of rates and taxes, should be fully known by all who are involved in the process. From this knowledge, the case for educational expenditure from public funds can be more rationally argued.

5   To provide an incentive for economy

a LFM offers a tangible incentive to everybody to make sensible savings in the use of fuel, of materials and stationery, in postage and telephone calls, when the saving is directly available to the establishment itself.

b There is much greater incentive for school buildings to be made more open to the general public when the income from such use is directly available to the particular establishment.

Two further objectives, less widely proclaimed but sometimes heard, are:

6 **To put the responsibility for reducing public sector expenditure at the point of delivery.**

7 **To encourage the entrepreneurial spirit without which the British economy will decline.**

Questions for discussion

1 *What objectives would you wish to add to the above list? Do any seem to you to be considerably more or less important than others?*

2 *Before reading the rest of the book, can you, on the basis of your own experience, think of practical ways in which these objectives could be achieved?*

3 *After reading the rest of the book, return to this chapter and reconsider the extent to which the objectives suggested here appear to have been met in the experience of those who have taken part in pilot schemes.*

The scope of LFM

There is nothing fixed or final in what should be included in an LFM scheme. The position is evolving all the time. In the following analysis of inclusions and exclusions, the Cambridgeshire scheme has been followed, but, as the explanatory notes indicate, there are a number of possible variations and hotly-debated points.

A Excluded

1 CENTRAL COSTS OF EDUCATION OFFICES, OFFICERS, INSPECTORS, ADVISERS

a The school cannot control these costs and the only point in allocating such costs would be as an exercise to show the 'true cost' of running a school. It seems probable that this exercise will have to be undertaken as part of the Government's opting-out proposals.

b A not-too-serious suggestion that a school in financial distress might choose to dispense with a part of the central service (eg advisers!) not only sent a ripple of anxiety down the corridors of Shire Hall but also served to highlight the overall inspectorial responsibility retained by an LEA.

2 INSURANCES, DEBT CHARGES, CAPITAL PROGRAMMES

3 REORGANISATION AND REDUNDANCY COSTS
a The financial burden of having to carry a number of redeployed teachers on protected salaries could not be met from a school's normal allocation.

b An imaginative suggestion that a school which wanted to encourage early retirement for a teacher who did not qualify for enhancement through the LEA scheme, should pay the enhancement factor from LFM flexibility, was rejected.

4 HOME TO SCHOOL TRANSPORT
There is no reason why an enterprising school might not tender for part of its own transport service, in order to make the most effective use of its own minibus or coach, but LEA coordination does seem sensible, especially as the timetabling of bus services to many schools is complex and involves coordination with public service vehicles.

5 LONG-TERM SUPPLY COVER (ILLNESS AND MATERNITY) FOR TEACHERS, NOT ANCILLARY STAFF
a The financial impact of two or three long illnesses and maternity leaves could be devastating and is clearly outside the scope of the head's management.

b Participating schools negotiated a central pool, a hold-back from their expected supply cover allocation, from which an internal transfer is made to the school after the 6th complete week of absence, back-dated to the first day of absence.

c Credit is given at a standard supply rate, irrespective of the salary of the long-term absent teacher: a head away for seven weeks is worth no more to the school than an absent Main Grade teacher. If a senior member of staff is away for some time, this could cause problems if other teachers have to take on extra responsibilities. Senior teachers will probably not be on full time-table but the supply cover will be provided for full days, so the compensation to over-burdened staff may have to be in free time rather than extra money. There is probably some room for negotiation here.

6 BUILDING MAINTENANCE

a This is an area of disagreement. LEA property departments tend to assume that heads and governors would divert funds from this heading to 'educational' expenditure and thus bring about a serious deterioration in the decorative condition of the school, and, even, in some cases, endanger the health and safety of staff and pupils. Many heads feel that they do not have the technical expertise or time to make judgments on these matters. Others, usually those not yet in LFM schemes, are said to lie awake at night worrying about how they would replace the school roof in the event of a hurricane.

b Other heads take a different view on this matter, claiming that people actually working within a school are extremely sensitive to the decorative condition of their classrooms and would not allow this to be neglected. Some heads claim that they could get jobs done better and more quickly by their own local contacts than by going through the LEA channels of tendering. Property departments counter this by claiming that this could lead to shoddy workmanship and corruption (eg through unsupervised tendering practices).

c There seem to be two possible compromises:
- to hold back the bulk of the maintenance budget centrally but to allow local discretion over a small proportion, with work being done by local initiative (eg by parent volunteers), subject to LEA oversight and the satisfactory maintenance of health and safety standards.
- to appoint property bursars to be based in, say, a large secondary school and to have area surveyor responsibility for a group of schools, or other county council establishments within the area. Salary could be apportioned among the cluster of establishments on a predetermined basis (eg surface area) and the property bursar could be an active attached member of the school community, joining in the consultative and decision-making process in using the LFM funds available. S/he would need to have freedom of action in hiring contractors (safeguards?) and could work from an agreed schedule of rates to reduce paper-work. A pilot scheme exploring some of these possibilities, but so far outside the LFM scheme, is in operation in some Cambridgeshire schools.

7   PLAYING FIELDS MAINTENANCE

a The main arguments for and against the inclusion of playing fields in LFM are similar to those already mentioned for buildings. The problem of the cost of large equipment is a serious one for an individual or small school.

b Many heads say they do not like playing fields maintenance carried out by peripatetic teams and would prefer a groundsman of their own, answerable in line management to the head and governors of the particular school. On the other hand, teams are cost-effective.

c Some would like the flexibility of combining grounds maintenance with buildings maintenance and caretaking/cleaning functions eg by employing an 'odd-job man/gardener', with a flexible job-description enabling him to work on minor indoor repairs in the winter and do more work on grounds and fields in the summer months. Some heads feel very strongly that this is a particularly good example of the kind of flexibility and local decision-making which is said to be at the heart of LFM.

d The LEA has a responsibility to provide a cost-effective service to *all* its schools. The withdrawal of a few large schools from a team concept could undermine this.

8   SCHOOL MEALS

a Few heads seem to want to get caught up with the problems of organising their own catering arrangements, even though they may have reservations about the capacity of a centrally organised school meals service to respond to the needs of individual schools. Others are anxious lest losses on school meals could lead to reduced educational expenditure.

b Proponents of the inclusion of school meals within LFM argue that, if the cook were answerable to the head and governors, it might be easier to make the school dinner menus match up with the health education teaching within the curriculum. Some authorities already do this very successfully without the added incentive that LFM would bring.

c One Cambridgeshire secondary school has been allowed a measure of independence by appointing its own catering manager as an additional appointment to the existing school meals staff. His salary has to be found by improving the turnover in everday school meals and from the income generated by catering for outside functions held within the school. It is too soon to say if the scheme will be successful and, in any case, it may well be argued that the circumstances of the particular school are so unusual that the scheme could not be generalised. The Governors of the school (a voluntary controlled school) have agreed to underwrite any losses from private funds for a three year trial period.

d It seems probable that further Government legislation to put the school meals service out to competitive tender will add a new dimension to this particular issue.

9   IN-SERVICE TRAINING

a Although the INSET/TRIST provision is county-based and organised, some Cambridgeshire schools decided to use part of their available funds to allow staff to be supported for in-service training after their request for LEA funding had been rejected.

b The arrangements for GRIST have now altered the ground-rules. A possible development may be for schools to have the possibility of viring extra funds *into* in-service training but not to be allowed to vire GRIST money *out of* in-service training.

10   MIDDAY SUPERVISION

a These schemes are normally subject to DES Educational Support Grant funding and this makes virement out of them very difficult.

b Some schools may want to add extra funds for midday supervision at particular times of the year.

c One Cambridgeshire school was allowed to fix its own rates of pay for midday supervisors within the total budget available to the school. It was not allowed, however, to keep and re-apply the underspend which accrued through its inability to recruit supervisors.

B Included

The following categories are usually included in LFM schemes, although here too there is room for debate. The explanatory notes draw attention to some of the aspects which may need particular attention and indicate areas of potential 'saving'. Two general notes about the use of 'savings' need to be made here:

• Money can be moved (virement) from any heading to any other in most schemes. Some LEAs require heads to give advance notice of major virements; in most cases, virement occurs by counter-balancing underspends and overspends.

• It is essential that over- and underspends are carried forward from one financial year to the next, usually as a global figure which can be redistributed as appropriate.

It has generally been found that the margin of flexibility is in the range of 1%–3% of total budget. This may not seem very much to those who have as yet had no experience of LFM but as it means, in cash terms, anything between £5000 and £45 000, depending on the size of your school, it is sufficient to enable useful action to take place.

1   TEACHER STAFFING

a There is no flexibility to alter national rates of pay but, in some schemes, Governors are allowed to offer more scale points than the normal allocation under Burnham. It remains to be seen how much flexibility LEAs will allow to schools as the new incentive allowances come into effect.

b Terms and conditions of service under the 1265 hours legislation are now much more tightly controlled and LFM cannot over-rule that.

c The mismatch of financial and academic year demands careful attention to detail in calculating a teaching staff budget eg 5/12ths of a year on one incremental point plus 7/12ths on the next incremental point. It is also important to remember to add the costs of superannuation and national insurance. The LEA can supply the formula and may even supply a computer program to do it for you.

d The deliberate appointment of teachers low down on the salary scale is an issue which has to be faced. Under the historical budgeting process, any advantage gained by such a policy was short-lived as the financial base was adjusted annually on the basis of the staff actually in post. The temptation to save in this way will be greater under formula budgeting (see later, page 21). LFM pilot heads confirm that educational considerations have in fact always overriden financial considerations in appointment procedures. To appoint a less satisfactory teacher on grounds of cheapness could be a recipe for disaster. As a watch-dog on this issue, it is good practice for appointing panels to include a governor and a deputy head and/or head of department as well as the head.

e The partial replacement of teachers leaving towards the end of the academic year has been one of the main ways of economising in this area. Secondary schools with a large number of examination groups, untaught from June to August, can make a saving here but care must be taken not to increase unduly the exam invigilation burden on the remaining staff. This is usually acceptable if the saving can be seen to be re-applied to the general benefit of the teaching staff, for example, by appointing extra ancillary staff to relieve teachers of some administrative chores, or by employing more supply staff.

f The combination of LFM and the new conditions of service offers interesting possibilities on the border-line of teaching time and teaching support time. It is possible to calculate the average teaching staff cost of one timetabled lesson for the whole year. It might be possible for a group of staff with reduced timetables, eg Heads of Year teaching, say, 28 periods out of 40, rather than the normal load of 35/40 — to agree collectively to teach an extra two periods each and to have the 'savings' applied specifically to extra ancillary help for themselves.

g In order to offer a safeguard to teaching staff, it seems likely that an LEA will specify a minimum staffing figure for each school. Lack of flexibility on this heading, which usually accounts for 75% of the costs of running a school, naturally limits the scope of management.

h It is necessary to determine with the LEA whether or not, in the event of a teachers' strike, the unpaid salary stays within the school budget or is taken into the centre. The likelihood of maverick heads fomenting militancy in order to balance the books should be discounted!

2   SUPPLY COVER

a Long-term absence and maternity leave are excluded.

b The new regulations for supply cover leave little room for man-oeuvre but it might be possible to negotiate with staff a local arrangement, such as an agreement to call in supply staff before day 3 if there are a lot of teachers away ill, but not to call in supply cover after day 3 if the staff are not under pressure. The need for accurate logging of absence and cover is vital to reassure staff that this kind of flexible local arrangement is designed to help them and not exploit them.

3   ANCILLARY STAFF

a The same rules about national pay-scales apply, as with teachers.

b Some schools in LEAs which do not operate a supply cover scheme for absent ancillary staff have created their own contingency pool to meet this need.

c Some schools have operated a scheme to bring in occasional extra ancillary help to ease the administrative burden at particular pressure points during the school year.

d In estimating the cost of ancillary staff in budget preparation, remember the on-costs, which are not the same as those under the teaching staff heading.

e The rates of overtime may be different for full-time and part-time staff.

4   CARETAKERS AND CLEANERS

a When Cambridgeshire chose to put half its cleaning out to private contract, the LFM schools were given the option of retaining direct labour, on new terms, at a cost no greater than the private contract would have been. This may not be possible under the new competitive tendering legislation.

b As there is no power to improve on union-negotiated rates of pay, some schools have had difficulty in recruiting cleaners. The virement option allows for money 'saved' on cleaning wages to be used to improve the cleaning equipment for such cleaners as can be appointed. It is ironic that, in cases where pay rates could be improved, union rules have been a source of inflexibility.

c Some schools have had to recruit pupils as paid cleaners. As they are paid at slightly lower rates, this has produced savings.

5   RENT AND RATES

a This was one of the few areas of the Cambridgeshire pilot scheme which produced serious disagreement between officers/councillors and heads/chairmen of governors. The former insisted on their inclusion on the grounds that they are part of the real cost of running a school. The latter group maintained that rent and rates were beyond the scope of a head's management, especially as nobody seemed totally clear about how a school's rateable value is determined. In any case, it is a question of internal transfer of funds within the County Council budget since the County Council levies the rates in the first place and then pays them back to itself.

b One of the few 'horror stories' of the pilot scheme occurred when one of the schools was re-rated in the course of a year and had to find an extra £12 000. The school was allowed to pay off the extra cost over four years but the resentment felt by the school concerned was shared by all those in the scheme. The key issue here is the extent to which the LEA should retain reserve funds to meet such unexpected mid-year crises.

c Later versions of LFM recognise the unfairness of the above experience and it is proposed that overspends or underspends on the rates heading should be cancelled out at the end of the financial year. A simpler solution may be to transfer them to the list of exclusions.

d One area of potential difficulty over rates is a privately funded building project — a PTA-sponsored sports pavilion. This would increase the rateable value of the site; who would pay the extra costs?

6   FUEL AND WATER
   a This is one of the most obvious target areas for sensible saving. A whole school policy of turning off unneeded lights, closing windows in cold weather and not allowing taps to run, can produce small but useful savings. Ideally, such a policy needs to be explained to all the pupils, along with the reason behind it, possibly stiffened by an incentive for pupils — extra social amenities, if targets are met.

   b The inclusion of fuel and water in LFM focuses attention on the need for efficient equipment — thermostats that really do work.

   c This also raises the question of energy conservation policies. Most LEAs have a department dealing with energy conservation. If a school decides to undertake energy conservation on its own initiative, it needs to agree with the LEA in advance that the base budget for fuel will not be changed, otherwise there is no incentive for energy conservation.

   d If water is metered, and especially where sewerage charges are linked to water consumption, it is worth considering the installation of more sophisticated devices for the flushing of boys' urinals. In many schools, these work on a mechanical method eg flushing every 20 minutes, night and day, all the year round. More sophisticated technology exists which allows for more frequent flushing during periods of high use and less frequent during the night, at weekends and in the holidays.

7   FURNITURE, FITTINGS, TEXTBOOKS, LIBRARY BOOKS, STATIONERY, MATERIALS, ADMINISTRATIVE, EDUCATIONAL AND DOMESTIC EQUIPMENT, PRINTING, OFFICE STATIONERY, POSTAGES AND TELEPHONES

a This large area of expenditure is grouped here for simplicity, although it is usually sub-divided on LEA printouts. It covers most of the areas of the traditional 'capitation' allocation. Many LEAs already allow unrestricted virement across these headings.

b The telephone bill for a large school can amount to 10% of all the expenditure under this heading. New equipment can be programmed to restrict the number of outside lines and to log calls made from each extension so that departments or pastoral teams can be 'charged back' for calls made.

c Most schools already operate accounting schemes for charging back to budget-holders the cost of postage, reprographics and so on. It can be argued that, if LFM is to be effective, the responsibility for careful use of resources has to be passed down the line of management to, say, Heads of Department. LFM has done away with the profligacy of spending 'their' (LEA) money since, under LFM, all money is 'ours' (the school's). The logical next step is for all members of the school community to have a greater sense of responsibility about spending the school's money. Incentives need to be passed down too.

d Some schemes restrict schools to purchasing a given percentage, usually 80%, from a central purchasing organisation. Some heads, especially of larger schools, find this frustrating. The issue is discussed more fully in Part 2, Chapter 6.

e Some schemes have been reluctant to employ the Hertfordshire cheque-book approach which seems to offer heads flexibility of suppliers and improved discount for rapid payment as well as cutting out some administrative procedures (ie coding and transfer of invoices to Shire Hall).

8 EXAMINATION FEES

a The inclusion of this heading is hotly debated on the grounds that an examination entry policy eg, eight subjects per 5th year pupil, ought to be determined by the LEA and directly funded by the LEA on the basis of the actual number of 5th Year, 6th Year and 7th Year pupils in the school.

b Given the relatively high cost of exam entries (more than twice what is usually spent on books and equipment for the year group concerned), schools with an above average intake are at a financial disadvantage in any county averaged scheme. On the frequently used argument of 'taking the rough with the smooth', it is said that schools with a below average intake have other problems which might be alleviated if they could use the money saved by having a smaller exam entry — for example, on more generous provision of equipment and materials for activity courses for non-exam pupils.

c If a department decides to enter candidates for a more expensive board, should it pay the extra cost?

9 EDUCATIONAL VISITS

If educational visits are seen as part of the extended curriculum, it is logical that this should be included within LFM flexibility. However, the question of raising a direct levy income from parents to set against this cost may be embodied in future legislation and this heading has to be noted as a grey area.

10 STAFF TRAVELLING AND SUBSISTENCE EXPENSES

a This heading mainly covers expenses incurred in teachers attending parents' evenings. For some years, because of industrial action, a small saving has been achieved. The '1265 hours' contractual arrangements will enable Heads to budget much more accurately for this in future.

b An example of how LFM flexibility can be turned to everybody's advantage comes from the school with its own catering service mentioned above (p.10). On parents' consultation evenings, teachers who do not wish to go home between 4 pm and 6.30 are provided with a good evening meal by the caterer, paid for out of the subsistence account. The caterer is pleased to have the customers; the amount paid is less than the travelling and subsistence allowance would have been (so the school account benefits) and, most important, teaching staff time and energy are saved by not having to do battle with rush-hour traffic.

11   ADVERTISING EXPENSES, CANDIDATES' INTERVIEW EXPENSES
a Flexibility to advertise more widely or more strikingly for posts difficult to fill has been appreciated.

b A potential problem lies in allowing schools to place advertisements direct in the *Times Educational Supplement* at their own expense at a time when an LEA may have a redeployment policy.

c Heads may tend to think more carefully before calling to an interview in Dover a border-line candidate living in Carlisle. This could disadvantage candidates in non-shortage subjects living in remote areas.

d An example of how LFM stimulates the entrepreneurial spirit comes from a school where members of staff with appropriate accommodation at home have made this available on an occasional bed-and-breakfast basis for interview candidates, at a rate which is below the normal LEA figure. Candidates are generally happy to be somewhere more personal than a hotel, the school saves money and the bed-and-breakfast entrepreneur makes a small profit.

e An item not currently included under this heading but which might have to be considered for the future is the question of relocation expenses for staff who have to move house to take up a new job. Could this not be said to fall legitimately within the LFM discretion of an individual school experiencing difficulty in recruiting in shortage subjects?

12   INCOME
a Income from events put on in the school buildings is credited to the school's account. After transfer of agreed sums for caretaker's overtime and for heating, the profit remains with the school.

b This clearly gives a financial incentive for schools to make their premises available but also encourages them to think more realistically about which rooms to open on a given evening. Unless heating systems are zoned, it could cost more to open the school for one booking than the school receives from the letting. The computerisation of heating systems will help.

c Many LEAs still require schools to make buildings available for LEA purposes, such as training sessions for governors, without charge to the LEA as hirer. It could be argued that if LFM aims to make schools more aware of real costs, the LEA should be similarly aware and should reimburse the school. The funds to cover this would have to be deducted from the total available to all schools before distribution, otherwise the LEA would not be able to pay the charges. This means that schools which are frequently used, because of their convenient position and suitable accommodation, would be less penalised than they are at present. Some LEAs have a collective agreement with the unions that they may use the premises free of charge, but perhaps even this needs to be reconsidered.

d Some LEAs issue a strict pricing schedule for room charges. Others allow greater flexibility, giving individual schools the freedom to charge a cost-only figure to, say, a local charity for a fund-raising event, while charging more heavily for a trade exhibition in the assembly hall, a caravan weekend on the playing field or a wedding reception in the school dining hall.

13   COMMUNITY AND ADULT EDUCATION, YOUTH SERVICE

a Traditionally, most LEAs have provided funding for this sector of their work from a different pocket from schools' funding. The logic of LFM, that is, the flexibility to respond to local needs, suggests that community and adult education should be incorporated. After all, it is very difficult to apportion certain building costs between evening and daytime use — who wears out the sports hall floor more quickly?

b In areas where community education and LFM have been brought together, a careful examination of costs has revealed previously undetected subsidies from one sector to the other. Telephone use, already referred to above in a different context, is cited as an example.

c While there are many good administrative and management reasons for bringing community and adult education into LFM, there are also major problems when it comes to putting on courses, eg for the unemployed, which attract little or no income. Social priority and financial incentive may be in conflict. This difficult area will be treated more fully in Part 2, Chapter 5.

Distributing resources to schools

Most of Part One of this book is taken up with showing how schools may go about making the best use of the money allocated to them. Before that is considered in detail, preliminary consideration needs to be given to the way in which the *amount* of money allocated to them is decided.

Although there is wide agreement that LFM offers management flexibility, there is considerable disagreement about *how* resources should be distributed to schools. This is nothing new; there have always been differences of opinion on this matter, but the effect of LFM has been to bring these differences out into the open for a more public discussion. This topic will be discussed in much more detail in Chapters 6, 7 and 8 of Part Two but an introductory explanation of the main issues is needed at this point.

In essence, the controversy is about whether money should be allocated on a *historical* basis or on a *formula* basis, or on a mixture of the two. There are different points of view on how the formula should be devised, depending on the size of school the protagonists work in.

Historical budgeting

The traditional way of allocating resources to schools is to calculate separately how much could be spent on each heading: teaching, non-teaching, fuel, caretaking etc. In the days before LFM, heads were told their allocations mainly in terms of the number of people they were allowed to appoint. Cash figures were usually only given in relation to 'capitation' (books, equipment etc). LFM converted staffing numbers into cash totals and gave virement and flexibility but in the early days, the sub-totals were still calculated on a historical basis.

So, for example, the teaching staff budget was based on the actual cost of the teachers in post at August 31st of the year before the budget year. Teaching staff establishments were revised from 1st September in line with predicted changes in pupil numbers. The exact figure was usually arrived at by a process of negotiation with an area officer who would have an element of discretion to respond to particular needs, depending on the urgency/stridency of the request for special consideration. When the revised establishment was known, deductions or additions were made on the basis of an average teacher's salary. A turnover factor (usually between 2½% and 1½%) was deducted from the total, based on the assumption that new teachers will be younger than departing teachers. The figure could only be calculated after the new staff had been appointed and so was always likely to be a year out of date. As the turnover was calculated at LEA level, there was bound to be an element of 'rough justice' at individual school level, with some gaining and others losing.

Other, similar examples included:

- ancillary staff established by a points scheme, related to pupil numbers, with the budget based on the actual cost of staff employed at a particular date. Turnover was also applied to this heading until it was discovered that ancillary staff are much more stable than teaching staff;
- cleaning and caretaking staff requirements based upon the floor area of the school;
- fuel costs based upon the previous year's consumption;
- supplies and services ('capitation') based on the anticipated number of pupils in each age-band on roll in January, adjusted when the actual January numbers were known.

Historical budgeting is a time-consuming operation, is susceptible to lobbying, runs the risk of giving schools special consideration long after the special need has ceased to exist and, most strikingly, produces enormous discrepancies in per capita expenditure, even between schools of similar size, with similar buildings and in similar social circumstances.

Formula budgeting

The term 'formula budgeting' is used to refer to the concept of distributing as much of the financial resources as possible according to a simple general formula. The crudest formula possible would be simply to relate allocation directly to the number of pupils in the school, thus giving a school of 1000 pupils twice as much money as a school of 500 pupils. This *reductio ad absurdum* example would clearly bring massive injustice since there are certain inevitable establishment costs involved in running any school, irrespective of size. A simple solution to this problem would be to give every school a lump sum, and then use formula on top of that.

A second reason why a direct relationship between pupil numbers and resource allocation would be unacceptable is that it has traditionally been accepted that pupils become more expensive to educate as they get older (smaller set sizes, more expensive books, exam entry fees, more equipment etc). This suggests that a formula should be weighted to recognise the number of pupils in each year group in a school.

Much of the discussion about the exact nature of the formula centres on the small school versus large school factor. If pupils in a small school are going to have a similar curriculum to those in a larger school, there will need to be a weighting in favour of the smaller school. The protection of the curriculum offer to pupils leads to a proposal known as curriculum-led staffing.

Running a school is not just a question of the teacher in the classroom. The administrative and pastoral system takes up 20% of the teacher time available; what are the different pressures on this aspect in smaller and larger schools? The heads of small schools maintain that much of the head's work is independent of the size of the school: attendance at meetings, producing publications and policies, working on the budget. Heads of large schools claim that the sheer number of pupils to be looked after increases the stress and workload for senior staff. They point out that, under the Burnham points allocation system, a much higher proportion of staff in small schools were on a promoted post and that people at Head of Department level, for example, have far fewer colleagues to look after for a Scale 4 allowance than heads of department in a much larger school on the same scale. Establishing a balance between these two points of view is difficult. Experience suggests that a formula needs to be devised which recognises the curricular needs of small secondary schools (500–800 pupils) and the administrative burdens of large schools (above 1400).

Balance and safeguards

The typically British spirit of determination and compromise has produced a solution, explained more fully in Part 2, Chapter 6, in which premises-related costs are distributed on a historical basis (which recognises that school buildings are in very different states of repair) but the remainder of the budget is distributed by formula. A simple formula would be insensitive to schools' individual needs; a complex formula would be bureaucratically expensive. Ultimately, elected councillors have to make the decision on which approach to adopt.

When you move from one system of budgeting to another, there are bound to be significant changes for individual schools. The ones currently underfunded will rejoice in their new-found affluence and will have no difficulty in finding ways of spending; those who experience a sharp reduction in resources will not be able to cope. The concept of *phased change* helps to soften the blow, by ensuring, for example, that any change will be reduced by 50% in the first year of a new system and that any year-on-year change in total available to a school, excluding inflation, will not vary by more than 5%.

LFM in operation

This section describes how LFM works in practice and offers some detailed examples of how certain problems can be overcome. Different strategies and approaches can be found in some of the contributions in Part 2. These differences highlight the individuality of LFM: different schools find slightly different ways of working the concept out in practice.

1 The financial cycle

Knowing what decisions have to be made at what time and preparing the consultative documents at the appropriate moment are central to effective management of LFM. This chart shows the relationship between the LEA cycle and the in-school cycle.

County Council budgeting process

July	The Medium Term Plan is approved by the Council. The first year of this plan forms the basis of the next year's budget.
August	Budget guidelines are issued detailing the cash limits within which each committee's estimates must be prepared.
September October November }	The Education HQ staff and Area Education Offices prepare the draft estimates for the Education Committee.
December	Education General Purposes sub-committee approves the estimates.
December	Central Government announces the Rate Support Grant to local councils. Estimates or policy need to be revised at this stage to take account of changes in grant.
January February }	Education Committee approves estimates. The County Council agrees the budget and fixes the rate precept.
March	**The Education HQ inform schools of total budget available for the coming year.**
April	New financial year begins.
April/May	Education HQ work on March closedown figures for preceding year.
June	**Schools receive final statement of underspend/overspend from preceding year.**

School financial cycle

February	By this stage, ideas about hoped-for curriculum changes for the following academic year should be firmed up with a cost factor included. Likely numbers in each year group, target set-sizes etc

need to be known. This makes early decisions on Year 4 options and, where relevant, 6th form returners, more critical. A contingency factor must be allowed for.

March   Likely under/overspend from current year is notified by LEA – to be taken into consideration in budget planning.

April/May   Once the figure for the financial year just started is known, detailed budget preparation proceeds (see below).

June   Budget for the year is finalised and adjusted when the final underspend/overspend from preceding year is confirmed.

September   Budgetary control printouts received each month and a check is kept on progress. Contingency budget used as appropriate. Careful monitoring but no major decisions.

Preparing the budget within school

In some LEAs, the finance department offers a proposed budget based on the expenditure pattern of the individual school for the preceding year. This gives a very useful starting point. Other LEAs simply give a global figure. This appears daunting at first but it becomes much easier once you become involved in the process. The following suggestions – offered as from one head to another – may prove helpful.

1   Confirm with the LEA the price base on which their global figure is based. If, as is likely, it is November of the preceding year, you must remain consistent to that figure, knowing that inflation will be added subsequently. If you ignore this first step, you can waste a lot of time working from different starting-points!

2   Write down the fixed charges such as rates, which the LEA will have sent you.

3   Next tackle the premises costs. You know, for instance, that the premises have to be heated so write down what you spent last year, unless you are aware of major changes which have taken place.

4   The premises have to be cleaned so next add in the figures from last year for cleaning and caretaking, looking back to the March printout to give you the closest indication of what you actually spent.

5   Next add in the relatively minor items like staff travelling, subsistence, interview expenses. Use last year's figure as a guide.

6   Make an inspired guess about the income you are likely to generate from the use of the premises. Start from last year's figure and remember that this is to be *added* to the total figure the LEA gave you at the beginning of the process.

7   Supply cover could be done next. Ask the LEA what figure they have used as the average daily cost of a supply teacher. Look back at the figures for your school for the preceding year and use them as a starter, '2 days per member of staff × £60.'

8   The LEA may well have notified you of the per capita figure they have used in generating the budget for 'capitation' expenditure. Armed with the accurate figures you have been working on in February, set aside an appropriate sum.

9   Now you are coming to the more difficult part: salaries. Start with the ancillary staff: you know what they are being paid; check on their incremental position, remember to add the on-cost (ask the LEA for this, usually about 11%) and this gives you an initial figure. If you have already decided to change the structure of the ancillary staff, amend your figure accordingly.

10   Teaching staff salaries represent probably 75% of your budget and are your most difficult problem. Work closely with your Director of Studies or curriculum Deputy. He or she will already have provided you with the draft curriculum for the coming year with the number of teaching periods required to staff it. Add to that the teaching support time, or non-contact time (usually 25%), divide by the number of periods in the school week and you have a target staffing figure. Take the existing staff and roll forward their salaries to next year, not forgetting increments and 'on-costs' (national insurance and employers' superannuation contributions, usually coming to about 16.25% in all). Delete those who are known to be leaving in August but remember that they will still be here for 5/12ths of the financial year. Add in the anticipated salaries of any new staff appointments (7/12ths). This process will give you your first notional teaching staff cost.

11   At this stage put in a contingency figure. Experience suggests ½% of total is about right.

12   Hold your breath while you, or, even better, your computer program, adds up all the totals you have produced for the separate headings. You will be relieved to find that you are not very far off what you have been allocated by the LEA.

13   You will have to make adjustments, of course, and this is where the costed alternatives must be discussed thoroughly through the consultative procedures (see page 30). Produce the first of what will be several drafts, making sure you label each successive draft clearly, for example,

This is what the school will look like next year for £x. We have been allocated £y by the LEA. The difference is + or −£z. Here are a number of different ways in which we can reduce/increase expenditure:
   a   Increase/reduce teaching staff by x teachers at an average salary of £y. This is how the curriculum could be affected . . .

b Increase/reduce ancillary staff by x hours at £y per hour. The effects would be . . .
c Increase/reduce capitation by a factor of x% producing a saving of . . . and so on.

14   Gradually the discussion focuses on the alternatives and eventually a consensus emerges, hopefully by early in May. You can now confirm/amend the provisional departmental capitation figures you have already discussed with heads of department.

15   As further appointments take place during May and June, keep a careful note of how these affect your total budget. If the appointments turn out to be slightly older than average, this will be a first call on your contingency budget; on the other hand, slightly younger than average appointments will give you a little more latitude in your contingency budget later in the year. You can be sure you will not be short of ideas for spending it!

16   By June, perhaps earlier, you will have received the final confirmation of the underspend or overspend carried forward from the previous year. You are now in a position to do some fine-tuning eg by making extra capitation available to departments or by praying for a mild winter!

17   Once the work on the budget is completed and confirmed with the LEA, there is very little you can do except monitor expenditure by means of the monthly printouts.Some minor corrective action may be possible but a major re-structuring of activities in mid-year is unlikely. A further example of the budget creation process is given in Part Two, Chapter 4.

Budgetary control

The LEA provides monthly printouts which should enable the head and governors to monitor expenditure and take minor corrective action, as required. Much of the success of the scheme depends on the accuracy and clarity of these tabulations and a great deal of work is being done to improve this essential tool in the effective implementation of LFM. Inevitably, mistakes will occur but these must be kept to a minimum and must be followed up until they are corrected.

The tabulations used in the Cambridgeshire pilot scheme are shown opposite and on page 28.

Cambridgeshire LFM Scheme – Schools
Expenditure and Income for the period ended August 1987

004 Huntgon Hinchinbrke

	Revised Total Budget for year £	Expected to date £	Actual to date £	Variation to date £
Employees				
0110 Full Time Teachers	1,425,421	600,100	586,655.56	13,444.44 –
0112 Casual Supply Tchrs	13,027	5,392	7,109.85	1,717.85
0114 GCSE Inset Funds	5,248	3,148	1,027.16	2,120.84 –
0120 Support Staff	96,935	40,467	33,148.73	7,318.27 –
0141 Caretakers	29,752	12,596	12,843.16	247.16
0142 Cleaners	36,000	15,228	14,152.88	1,075.12
0179 For Lang Assts etc	7,733	1,534	1,136.64	397.36 –
	1,614,116	678,465	656,073.98	22,391.02 –
Premises				
1118 Alterations-LFM Schs	2,000	334	680.00	346.00
1320 Oil	23,635	9,049	9,147.92	98.92
1330 Electricity	30,000	10,050	9,002.40	1,047.60 –
1340 Gas-Mains	18,000	6,893	2,959.64	1,933.36 –
1341 Gas-Cylinders	1,600	523	1,166.01	643.01
1351 Water Charges	2,670	1,076	1,242.82	166.82

Cambridgeshire LFM Scheme – Schools *(continued)*
Expenditure and Income for the period ended August 1987

004 Huntgon Hinchinbrke

	Revised Total Budget for year £	Expected to date £	Actual to date £	Variation to date £
Premises				
1360 Cleaning Materials	7,120	2,725	5,061.13	2,336.13
1370 Window Cleaning	770	319	.00	319.00 –
1391 Refuse Collection	1,232	511	465.77	134.77
1540 General Rates	85,352	42,676	36,510.85	6,165.15 –
1541 Sewerage Rates	3,121	1,257	1,682.83	425.83
	175,500	75,413	68,099.37	7,313.63 –
Supplies & Services				
2600 Capitation Allownces	125,085	46,406	53,215.70	6,809.70
2990 Other Hired Services	1,500	622	1,350.00	728.00
	126,585	47,028	54,565.70	7,537.70
Transport & Mvble Pl				
3110 Car Allowances	3,028	1,262	761.80	500.20 –
	3,028	1,262	761.80	500.20 –

From left to right, the information given is:

1 *the detail code* (part of the accounting code describing the type of expenditure)

2 *a narrative description* of the detail code

3 *a revised total budget* for the year, i.e. the budget as specified by the school but with inflationary factors added (see later).

4 *the expected expenditure* to date. This figure is calculated according to a computer pattern for an 'average' school operating under 'normal' circumstances. This has produced a lot of confusion in the pilot scheme and is one of the areas where improvement is needed. Each school needs to be able to build up its own prediction of spending patterns.

5 *The actual expenditure* to date is the total of all expenditure on that item up to a given date, usually the end of the preceding month, about two or three weeks before the printout is received in school.

6 *The variation to date* column shows the difference between expected and actual, a minus figure indicating an underspend. In the pilot scheme, this last column was much agonised over, often to little purpose since the figures in the preceding two columns contained too many inaccuracies.

In addition, the school receives another tabulation of the detailed transactions that have taken place in the preceding month. This lists all payments and credits and it is this document which the school accounts staff need to cross-check carefully. Most of the frustrations of the pilot scheme arose from lack of information about why 'journal transfers' had been made. Plans to improve the computer program are under active consideration and this will streamline what can be a time-consuming and frustrating process.

Those setting up new schemes will learn a great deal from the frustrations of pilot schemes in this area of transmission of information. Many newcomers fear that this kind of checking will be beyond them, both in terms of time and expertise. There is no need for that to be so. With a properly designed computer program and, ideally, on-line access to the LEA mainframe computer, there is no reason why the process of checking should not be even easier than current manual methods.

The allocation of inflation is another major potential source of confusion. There is nothing more unnerving than to receive a monthly printout with your total budget changed without explanation. You feel as though you are involved in a game where the rules keep changing. People coming into new schemes need to press for clarification from the LEA Finance and Administrative section to determine which items are cash-limited, which items are inflation-indexed and at what point in the year will the inflation factor (or pay award) be added?

Another important point to be clarified at the outset is whether or not inflation is added to the budget *as prepared by the school*, or whether it is added *on the basis of an LEA average*. It is more likely to be the latter method; the former could lead an LEA into serious trouble if all schools decided to allocate increased expenditure to the heading most likely to receive the highest inflation factor. From the school's point of view, it is also advisable that the 'contingency heading' referred to above in the explanation of the budget preparation process, should be attributed to one of the named headings rather than coded separately; if coded separately, it may well not receive any inflation factor at all!

LFM: responsibility and participation

The implementation of LFM disturbs the normal channels of communication between school and LEA as well as within school itself. It also disrupts the established patterns of responsibility. At LEA level, for example, in a large county with area offices, what precise function do these offices have when each school receives its budget direct from the centre and has responsibility for its use? This, and other LEA implications, will be considered in Part 2, Chapter 7. Although LFM is about flexibility of individual establishment response, there is a great deal for schools to learn from each other in how to manage LFM freedom most effectively. Ways in which this can be done will be discussed in Part 2, Chapter 5. This chapter concentrates specifically on responsibility and participation within school.

In-school consultation

LFM schemes usually specify that responsibility for the school's finances lies with the *governors*, although the management lies with the *head*. The Government's consultation papers vacillate on this point and it is a matter which needs clarification. Clear lines of communication, consultation and decision-making need to be built in to LFM. At its best, it increases the level of participation within the school community; at its worst, it could be highly divisive.

In the Cambridgeshire Pilot Scheme and in the generalised scheme, the LEA insisted that all schools should set up consultative procedures and it is interesting to note that there were slight variations between them. What follows is one example of a Financial Management Committee constitution from a secondary school, with explanatory notes. (Another example, with fuller discussion is given in Part 2, Chapter 4.)

FINANCIAL MANAGEMENT COMMITTEE

Terms of reference
The Committee will serve as an advisory body to the Governors. Recommendations to be made to the Governors will be formed following full consultation with interested parties, including teaching staff, support staff and parents.

[*This makes it quite clear that the final decision on any contentious issue lies with the full Governing Body. The Financial Management Committee is nevertheless highly influential.*]

Composition of Committee
The Committee will consist of:

a Five Governors to include: Chairman of Governors
Chairman of Governors' Finance Commitee
[*This is a voluntary controlled school with its own Trust Fund.*]
Parent Governor
Teacher Governor
plus one other Governor.

b Three ex-officio members of staff: The Head
The Deputy Head i/c Finance.
The Senior Accounts assistant.

c Four elected members of the teaching staff.
d One elected member of the non-teaching staff.
e The clerk to the governors.

In addition, the Committee may, from time to time, co-opt members with particular expertise. [*This was added so that a senior member of staff like the Director of Studies could be called in to advise on curricular implications of financial decisions.*]

Election of school-based staff
Teaching staff
In the first instance, four members of teaching staff will be elected by teaching colleagues using a system of single transferable voting. The two who receive the majority of votes will serve for two years. The other two will serve for a period of one year.

[*December is recommended as the best month for elections so that new members have time to settle in before the budget creation process starts. The decision to have direct elections among all staff rather than to have union-specific representatives had been taken after a full staff discussion and referendum.*]

Non-teaching staff
One member of the non-teaching staff will be elected bi-annually to serve for a period of two years. Eligibility for re-election and the procedure for the filling of vacancies will be as for the teaching staff.

Process of consultation
i The responsibility for the consultative arrangements and their effective working is the head's and the Governing Body's.

ii It shall be the responsibility of the Financial Management Committee to consult fully with concerned parties before forwarding recommendations to the Governing Body.

iii Consultation has to be understood as being more than giving information. It must allow for time for information given to be considered and for views to be expressed. This is especially important when decisions are being made to increase or reduce the school's provision in a particular area.

iv Teaching and non-teaching members of the FMC may attend the Heads of Department meeting when curricular changes are being considered.

v Consultation with parents, pupils and the local community may be appropriate on particular issues and will need to be considered. [*This has not happened as yet.*]

vi Individuals or groups within the school will be able to raise issues or ask for consultation through their elected representatives.

Participation

The participation of governors and staff is encapsulated in the preceding section. It is not so easy to specify how parents (other than through the parent governor) and pupils can become involved.

Some schools have tried the following ideas:

● reporting regularly to parents via bulletins about the school's financial situation (this is now enshrined in the annual report requirements).

● holding special PTA meetings to explain LFM.

● letting parents know exactly what is available per pupil to spend on books and equipment, in the context of wider fund-raising efforts.

● giving pupils clear and specific instructions about fuel economy, with the incentive of social amenity improvements for good performance.

● giving elected school councils responsibility for a sum of money to be spent at their discretion on amenities for pupils. The money would come either from LFM funds or from privately raised funds. There is some evidence to suggest that this approach encourages good housekeeping and increases financial awareness.

● using the annual parents' meeting as an occasion to encourage parental interest in the topic.

Reservations about LFM

It seems probable that LFM schemes will expand over the next few years, either on the basis of their perceived advantages or because of central Government diktat. The responses to the Government's 1987 consultation paper suggest less opposition to LFM than to many of the other proposals. Nevertheless, it would be unwise to ignore the objections which are being made and the reservations which are being expressed in a number of quarters. The list below is a compendium of views expressed in newspaper and journal articles, in broadcasts and in conferences and seminars held in various parts of the country. (An indication of some of the more specific sources can be found in the annotated bibliography on page 166).

Many of the reservations are inter-related but, for the sake of ease of reference, they have been grouped under a number of broad headings. They are not listed in any particular order of importance, nor does their inclusion indicate that the editor of this volume agrees with them.

1 THE CHANGING ROLE OF THE LEA

a LFM will be used by elected members as a way of passing on to governors and heads unpleasant decisions about where economies are to be made.

b LFM is primarily a political stratagem designed to destroy local government and, by creating wide differences between schools, to destroy the comprehensive system.

c LFM does not save money; it has been shown that it increases staff required at LEA office level.

d The LEA will have opportunities to make disguised cuts in provision eg by making inadequate inflation allowances. How can differential levels of inflation be made without resorting to an agreed standard level of provision, which defeats one of the objects of LFM?

e The weakening of the LEA role will undermine authority-wide curriculum development.

f Elected members need to recognise that LFM cannot be done on the cheap; are they prepared to regard it as a priority in competing for scarce resources?

2 THE EFFECT ON THE HEAD

a The head's energies will be diverted away from the 'real work' of the school into even more administration. The head will have less time for teaching and school staff respond better to being led by somebody who demonstrates skills relevant to education rather than somebody appointed for possession of the skills of accountancy.

b The range of skills demanded of a head is already wide enough without adding financial wizardry, negotiating with the local workforce, entrepreneurialism and building maintenance knowledge, to mention but four.

c Heads will need specific training for LFM (and deserve extra payment for the increased responsibility).

d Heads are being asked to take on too many innovations simultaneously. Already struggling with GCSE, TVEI, extension, new conditions of service, new articles of government, records of achievement, appraisal, GRIST, the national curriculum, CPVE and AS Levels, it is totally unrealistic to expect them to cope with LFM as well.

e Heads are already too powerful and extending their financial control will exacerbate the situation.

f Teaching heads in small primary schools cannot possibly be expected to take on LFM on top of their existing load, and certainly not without extra ancillary help.

g Heads will be appointed for their skills as accountants and fund-raisers rather than their educational experience. This will become even more marked as parents have the majority vote on Governing Bodies and will be aggravated by the Government's intention to withdraw LEA guidance from the appointment of heads.

h Some heads fear the legal implications of the system and foresee the possibility of personal litigation for failure to manage efficiently.

3   THE EFFECT ON TEACHING STAFF

a There will be prejudice against appointing older teachers because they will be more expensive than young ones.

b There will be an increased workload on senior staff immediately below the level of head because of all the extra work taken on by the head.

c Teachers will be open to exploitation: they may be put under pressure to contribute to economies on the supply cover budget by doing more than their fair share of cover; they will have to waste more time chasing up ways of making small economies; they might be expected to undertake minor maintenance; they will be expected to work in dirtier classrooms and in underheated buildings; above all, they will be subject to the pressure of divided loyalties because they will not want to be seen to be refusing to do things which would result in more money being available to spend on equipment for the children.

d There will be an increasing use of temporary appointments and promotions as heads seek to keep their financial options open. This will lead to an increasingly unsettled workforce.

4 THE EFFECT ON ANCILLARY STAFF
a Most schools are already under-provided for in the area of ancillary staff. Unless an LFM scheme allows for extra office help, the burden will be too great.

b Office staff will need special training, especially if, as seems likely and indeed essential, accounts and administration become computerised.

c Many smaller primary schools have only one ancillary who is already secretary, nurse, tea-lady etc. How can they expect to recruit people with accounting skills as well, especially at the salary level offered?

5 THE EFFECT ON GOVERNORS
a LFM will require governors to be much more closely involved in the detailed running of the school. Is this a time commitment they are prepared to take on?

b LFM will adversely affect the recruitment of governors and will tend to distort membership of Governing Bodies in favour of the middle-class bank-manager type, the unemployed or the recently retired.

c With an increased workload, governors should be entitled to claim travelling or attendance expenses and this would increase the costs of running the school.

6 THE EFFECT ON PARENTS
a Parents will come under increased pressure to raise extra funds to support their children's education.

b The stimulation of local fund-raising will disguise even further the present inadequate funding.

c There will be increased differences between schools as not all parents are equally willing or financially capable of contributing money to education.

7   THE EFFECT ON SCHOOLS AND PUPILS

a LFM, especially by formula distribution, will be particularly hard on schools which start from a low base, eg have antiquated heating systems, old furniture, or buildings which are vulnerable to burglary and arson.

b The pressure to use schools for commercial ventures may have a bad effect on the conditions under which pupils work.

c A formula based crudely on pupil numbers will result in gross inequity in the distribution of resources.

d Unless the LEA retains a significant 'safety-net', a school might find itself financially penalised by a failure elsewhere in the LEA service, for example if maintenance is managed separately, a serious mistake by that service could have serious financial repercussions for the school concerned.

8   THE EFFECT ON TEACHING UNIONS

a LFM will undermine the collective bargaining strength of the unions. Traditionally the bulk of negotiating has been carried out by the paid Union officers talking at central or LEA level. Under LFM, much more negotiation will need to take place at school level.

b This will increase the requirement for greater training for school-based union representatives. This, in turn, will increase costs as they will need time off to undertake this training.

c The need to organise this training, to provide information and back-up for union representatives in school and to adjust to new systems of communication will impose strain on an already over-worked union structure.

d LFM could lead to disparities of pay and conditions in individual schools. It will be difficult to organise effective industrial action on a school-by-school basis.

9   CRITICISM OF PILOT SCHEMES

a The pilot schemes were predestined to be successful because they included only, or mainly, keen volunteers. Once schools become involved in an experiment, the Hawthorn effect guarantees the success of the experiment.

b The evaluation of the pilot schemes has been inadequate and in particular there is no clear evidence that pupils have derived any benefit. Since schools exist for the education of pupils rather than as models of administrative efficiency, this is a glaring omission.

c The Inspectorate, both at LEA and at HMI level, has not been sufficiently involved in LFM evaluation.

d The pilot schemes have shown that LFM needs a great deal of officer attention. Once LFM becomes generalised, this attention will not be available.

Questions for discussion

1   *Do you, or members of the group with whom you are working, have any further initial reservations about LFM which are not mentioned above?*

2   *When you have read Part Two of this book, return to this chapter and reconsider the strength and weakness of the reservations made above.*

Part Two:
Personal Perspectives on LFM

Chapter 1 My hopes for Local Financial Management

John Brackenbury

In this introductory chapter to Part Two, John Brackenbury, one of the co-sponsors of the Cambridgeshire Pilot Scheme in 1982, reflects on why he was keen to see it established and what he saw as its potential for improving the educational opportunities for young people.

Schools and Local Education Authorities view themselves – and each other – very differently. The two perspectives are psychologically distinct, and have to do with the ways in which the two parties perceive one another. LEAs are often seen as conglomerate, faceless collections of bureaucrats, rarely identified with a single individual as schools always are with their headteachers. From a school the LEA is seen as 'them', different in quality from 'us' at the sharp end, the chalk-face, where the action is . . . From the Shire Hall perspective schools are characterised by the idiosyncrasies of each headteacher, and by their achievements or problems or both.

It is not usual for an LEA and its schools to have a unified vision of the common task, that of educating the pupils. The roles are different, always have been, and, supposedly, always will be. It seems to follow that the visions will also be distinct. Roughly speaking, the LEA provides – or doesn't provide; while the schools do the job as best they can with what they get – or don't get.

Built in to these tunnel visions are assumptions about the permanence of the way things happen. Introducing even a minor change – say, from shiny to soft toilet paper – can take ages; longer than it takes to change a headteacher, or to reform a ritual of comparable importance. Changing an administrative method can even take longer; this may partly account for the inherent reluctance of many to change anything at all – the fear of the interim as well as of the new unknown.

Local Financial Management in Cambridgeshire started about ten years ago with a scheme called Increased Financial Responsibility involving some 30 volunteer schools. The scheme allowed heads to switch expenditure between various categories of school requirements such as books, equipment, and interior decoration. It caused little or no stir, but it was a good beginning.

In November 1981 I put down a special motion for debate at the County Council meeting later that month. It read:

i that this Council instruct the Education Committee to investigate forthwith the feasibility of devolving financial responsibility for education expenditure to governing bodies of Colleges and Schools;
ii that a pilot scheme consisting of willing participants be instituted as soon as possible;
iii that the object initially and throughout the exercise be to secure the efficient education of the population of Cambridgeshire.

On 3 November Councillor Robert James, an originator of the Increased Financial Responsibility scheme, moved a recommendation at the Policy Committee . . .

. . . that the Education Committee be asked to consider more flexibility in the control of their finances in 1982/83 by giving authority to the Governors of secondary schools to control their own budgets within a total cash limit as established by the Council's budget where the accountancy backup is available from the Director of Finance and Administration. As a first stage the practice should be introduced in establishments where they have agreed to accept this responsibility.

The Policy Committee adopted the recommendation. In the debate at the Council meeting on 17 November 1981 the special motion was taken as an amendment to the Policy Committee recommendation; it was defeated. The recommendation was approved, and a few days later I gladly accepted an invitation to join Councillors Alan Ashton and Robert James on a steering committee to oversee the pilot scheme. I was pleased to have been a founder-member, and we worked amicably together.

Twenty years before, when Warden of Impington Village College, I had been trying for weeks to get the LEA to let me have half a laboratory assistant to make a whole one. Labs at Impington were dispersed and the existing half assistant was perpetually 'on safari' between them. Imagine my feelings when, just after my final plea had failed, there appeared, unannounced, a large tarmac spreader to resurface the College car-park – something that, in my view, was quite unnecessary. My exasperation was not relieved when I learnt, upon enquiry to Shire Hall, that the cost of resurfacing the car-park was about the same as the missing half's annual salary. I fumed, huffed and puffed, to no immediate avail – but, I remembered and, in the fulness of time, I had my reward. It was my firm belief then, later, and now that in most cases the person on the spot knows best; the half lab-assistant and the car-park was assuredly one such case.

In 1982 the pilot scheme was established with six secondary schools and one primary school, all of them volunteers. The Chief Education Officer took a keen interest in the development and his second deputy advised the steering committee, and kept it on course.

More important than the original details are the purpose and methodology of LFM in schools. The purpose is the enablement of better education for the learners in the schools. LFM is not, and never should be, an end in itself. The method has to match the purpose, that is to say it, too, must be educational. People engaged in LFM have to learn to understand one another and the system better, and to accept joint responsibility for working together to a common end. One of the unsung, unforeseen, and very valuable by-products of the pilot-scheme was the increase in mutual understanding of the Shire Hall people and the people in the schools. It didn't happen overnight; it took time and patience.

LFM pushes people to analyse the process, to explain it, and to co-operate in making it work. It has even precipitated a meeting or two to discuss the future of education and the part in that future that might be played by the LEA, which seems timely in view of the changes proposed by Secretary of State Kenneth Baker. LFM also adds a dimension to the function of governors and brings a new precision to their perspective. In pilot scheme papers the rubric always linked the governors and the head in a partnership of responsibility for expenditure plans; and it was a pleasure to see, at the periodic 'review and evaluation' meetings, the chairmen of governors sitting with their respective headteachers.

Participating schools found (and will find) that the practice of LFM induces the need to create instruments to enable it to work, and to work better. Such instruments have to be designed with three main functions in mind: first, to enable choices about expenditure to be explored by those affected; second, to enable the consequent recommendations to be made to the school's finance group; and third, for the governors-and-head to make decisions, in the light of the finance group's proposals, for the betterment of the education for which they are responsible.

The LEA sets the framework; allocates the total budgets; provides information to help the governors-and-head to make their decisions; and, by its monitoring procedures, encourages development and prevents mishaps.

LFM has its critics, and it would be idle to dismiss their criticism for they are mostly practitioners who, as I have argued, often know better, if not best. The important criticisms are about power, about time, and about passing the buck. It must be remarked that the Secretary of State's apparent adoption of LFM for instant deployment to the nation's schools will be more than enough to confirm its most sinister implications to some critics. It is to be hoped that such patronage does not confer the kiss of death upon local partnership.

The possible misuse of power is part of what is risked by conferring it. Every head is potentially a megalomaniac – fortunately, most remain refreshingly human and sane. Giving them a budget to distribute is giving them no more than parents have been willing to give to the principals of colleges of higher and further education, and what parents in the independent sector, whatever their motives, have been willing to entrust to heads of private schools, called public.

Greater freedom of choice in distributing resources within a prescribed total budget certainly enables more power than hitherto to be exercised; but even so it only starts to even up the balance between a head's large responsibilities and the commensurate power which should be available. Since in all properly-conducted LFM establishments, governors are to be responsible alongside the head, I see no reason why that access of power should be misused. Indeed, I would expect it to be used aright. Consultation is essential and this should mean thinking together about problems before their solution. If practised sincerely, it reaps its own reward in trust – insincerity is, evidently, profitless.

The use of time, the second resource, is rightly regarded as a professional concern of high importance. Some argue that heads are primarily teachers and should not be preoccupied with managing finance. They are there to run the schools, to discipline pupils, to vitalise staff, to keep order and to maximise learning by all possible means. Well, yes, and a great deal more besides, including their own teaching. Given initial help and continued back-up from the LEA, would not even the most starry-eyed educationist-head find her/his capability extended and enhanced? The isolation inseparable from lonely responsibility can be mitigated, to good effect, by the increased involvement of teachers, governors and parents, while the ability to divert some funds to in-school in-service training could go some way to enabling the refreshment of vitality deemed to be part of the head's available magic.

Prolonged preoccupation usually implies a lack of control of time and a misreading of priorities. LFM is but one of the means towards the end of better education. Heads will be found, and will find themselves, to be capable of taking in their stride the financial skills that many of their pupils already have, and may thereby add to their personal resources for leadership, of which management is an important strand.

It has been forcefully suggested that LFM is a trick by the LEA to shift responsibility for cuts in resources of staff and materials on to schools. If an LEA were that cynical the criticism would be deserved. It is a sad commentary upon the so-called partnership between LEAs and schools, a partnership which will have to do a lot better than that to withstand pressures from the new centralism. Such cynicism, like insincerity, is profitless and it need not persist. Only some such community of aim as is pointed to by LFM can break the destructive suspicion by each party of the other and enable schools and local authorities to enter more fully into fruitful partnership. Indeed the workings of the budgeting system must of necessity be more open to question and thus there is less likelihood of evasion of responsibilities on anyone's part.

It seems likely that LFM, in some form or other, will be part of forthcoming legislation. If so, it is to be hoped that those who decree it will have a care for what has been discovered locally, on the pulses and along the heart. However that may be, discerning readers will already have wondered what is likely to be the eventual function of LEAs. It looks as if the government intends to restrict the power of local authorities – first, by cutting the rate support grant, and second, by encouraging schools to secede from local authority control on a simple majority of parental votes. Some kind of distant control – since the money will still be public money – will presumably be established.

LFM as practised in Cambridgeshire rests upon good local under-standing. Many of the schools are community schools and more are likely to become so. There is thus already an established consensus about the importance of 'localness' in the county, which has been enhanced by the introduction, in Geoffrey Morris's administration of Cambridgeshire education, of LFM. It can be seen to be a logical development of Henry Morris's idea of Village Colleges, pioneered 60 years ago.

In such circumstances the function of the LEA can be more easily discerned than is perhaps the case with more remote or distanced partnerships in local education. First, the LEA appears as the bulwark against dictation and direction from a central control station of the education of the people.

Second, it is the guarantor of local communication. Just as LFM presupposes that the local people in the local school are best placed to decide how to spend public money on that particular school, so the LEA is best placed to exercise the control of the total resources available to the local educational establishments. Neither the DES nor the Secretary of State are conspicuous for their speed of response to, or sympathetic understanding of, a particular school's needs. A good local authority, on the other hand, is sensitive to what will work here, what there, and what over in that corner of the county. Morality of communication is best ensured by a positive will to inform and to be informed, with the ability to take quick and effective action if, and when, it is necessary.

Third, the LEA is the holder of local tradition. On more than one occasion since Henry Morris retired from the Cambridgeshire scene, there have been threats to the continued working of community education or to one or other of its community colleges – arising from lack of understanding of local feelings about local needs. The local authority in every case has 'kept quick the living hedge' that is the continuum of its responsibility.

Fourth, the LEA is accustomed to the job of running schools in partnership with them. The Secretary of State's role in the partnership envisaged by the Butler Act implies an understanding leadership and response to education. At present the LEA is doing this job, and, given its continued existence, will enable the central national administration to regain its own equilibrium, and to contribute more effectively to the national educational needs.

I have had the privilege of working closely with all the contributors to this book, and it will be for them to record their opinions, if they so wish, about the state of progress of LFM. They will, undoubtedly, illuminate other perspectives and bring their special experience to bear. I am delighted to have been invited to introduce this part of the book of which assuredly the best is yet to come.

I have often been amazed, since 1981, with the range and depth of the many interesting problems that have occurred in the course of the pilot scheme; far beyond either my experience or my expectations. I believe that LFM has within it the seeds of growth in development of educational understanding, beyond its immediate application; because it has, beside its financial aspect, incorporated both the localness of cooperation and the management that is essential to good leadership.

Questions for discussion

1 *Looking at the wording of the November 1981 motions proposed by John Brackenbury (lost) and by Robert James (passed), do you detect any significant differences of emphasis?*

2 *Why would John Brackenbury still face today the same problem as a Cambridgeshire LFM head in relation to the lab assistant and the tarmac? Do you consider the inclusion of some aspects of maintenance to be essential to the effectiveness of the scheme?*

3 *Can members of the discussion group contribute examples of administrative changes which have taken a disproportionately long time to bring about? Does the group agree that educational development has been hampered by 'the fear of the interim as well as of the unknown'?*

4 *One of John Brackenbury's major hopes is that finance can be a link to bring LEA officers and schools into genuine partnership. Discuss within the group the extent to which you feel schools and LEA officers to be operating in partnership or in opposition.*

5 *If you agree that LFM is a 1980s extension of the Henry Morris principle of community education, do you also feel that an LFM scheme which seeks to exclude community education is self-contradictory?*

6 *When you have read the rest of this book, return to John Brackenbury's chapter and assess the extent to which his original hopes have been fulfilled. What has happened of which he might disapprove?*

Chapter 2 A councillor and governor's view
Robert James

As co-sponsor with John Brackenbury of the Cambridgeshire Pilot Scheme and in view of his continuing work at the heart of the LFM scheme, Robert James is ideally placed to bring two particular perspectives: as an elected councillor, he has seen how LFM can change the roles of councillors and officers in an LEA; as a governor in one of the pilot schools, he has seen how the part played by governors in the life of the school can be developed by LFM. This hard-hitting and outspoken article concludes with an unashamed apologia for LFM.

Changing the rôle of the councillor

As Managing Director of a group of construction companies in Cambridge, and also a County Councillor, it was quite clear to me, right from the begining, that the ethos of management in a council was completely different from a commercial organisation. In fact, in those days, there was very little interest in management as such; it was assumed that everything could be achieved by pouring money into it. For a time this worked, but inevitably the bills came home in the 1970s and we have yet to recover.

It seemed to me at the time that little could be done; councillors as a whole have not come to serve as managers, but in the first case to look after the best interests of the people in their own electoral division. They do not look on themselves as directors of a large organisation with a multi-million pound budget, employing many thousands of people.

There seems to be a conviction among many councillors that you can only run an organisation satisfactorily if you are personally involved in the day-to-day minutiae of decision-making, rather than setting the policy direction for the officers to work through, and seeing to it that they work to the stated policies and achieve the expected results. Thus you find councillors getting themselves immersed in the detail and officers who either do not know where they are going or have their job overruled by the councillors. This applies equally to many other people who are involved in running the council's business, such as school governors.

Accepting the above, the problem was to work out how the local education authority could maintain control by elected members, who are ultimately responsible to the electorate, and let others concentrate on the daily minutiae – people who have a far better local knowledge than a county councillor or a central officer.

The computer solved this basic problem. It could provide detailed management information for any cost centre, and consequently could also provide the tool for central management to ensure that schools were operating within the overall policies laid down by the Education Authority.

Taking the plunge into LFM

Local Financial Management was the scheme devised as a practical possibility for achieving the above aims. The arrival of LFM had many spin-offs in addition to direct management in the school. It brought home to me, and to others, the pathetic lack of priority that the council had given to helping its staff to meet the aims it had itself set. Such a lack of understanding really amazed me, and as the scheme expanded we met uninformed, yet articulate, hostility again and again. This hostility is invariably based on a lack of understanding of management.

It seemed to me that there could be no excuse for not managing our officers on one hand, and, on the other, giving them the tools to do the job, on a much more logical basis. Looking at the various forces arrayed against this development, it was clear that there was a fundamental lack of understanding, even among those who were keen to have a go. There was a very real risk that the whole project would founder if it was allowed to be debated and planned for about two years before it was put into operation, as usually happens with any initiative in a democratic organisation. It was essential that the 'deep-end treatment' system was adopted. We therefore proceeded almost immediately with the handful of people who *were* keen to try it. In effect, we were designing a scheme on the experiences of those who were already trying to operate it – not exactly the way recommended by management services! Obviously, we would have liked to have had 12–18 months planning to bring this scheme in, and to get some key people trained, as would happen in any commercial organisation. This was not practical, not only because of the general hostility, but also because of the complete lack of any practical knowledge on the part of anybody concerned, so that training simply could not be done.

Powerful forces were trying to stop the scheme right up to the last minute. As I was standing down as council leader, and in any case there was an election a short while off, I was determined that it should proceed on an ad-hoc basis. I must say that the way the many staff members and governors rose to the occasion to get the scheme up and running was very satisfactory.

We well realised our failings, or at least thought we did, and in the event the problems were greater than we anticipated. To help solve them, we turned to outside help. Roger Duffet, from BP's Management Services Unit (brought in through the connection that the former warden of my Village College at Comberton had with BP, where he was trying to increase the co-operation between schools and industry) came for six weeks and looked at what we were trying to do, and also at the management of a few of our schools. Six weeks was a ridiculously short time, but he certainly confirmed my views of the inadequacy of the non-teaching management of our education service, particularly in its establishments. He really brought it home to us, and others, how backward we were. This is not to criticise the existing officers, rather it indicates a lack of coherent policy among members to keep up with modern methods.

One phrase which stuck in my mind, when talking about the responsibility of headteachers as far as general management for schools was concerned, was that they were not managers at all but only had the responsibility of a chief clerk. This was the authority we were giving to people in charge of our large establishments – spending, in many cases, more that £1m a year! It was not surprising that the general delivery of education was in such disarray.

When I started to think about the situation that LFM was uncovering, I could see quite plainly how we were failing. Those carrying responsibility in the schools were almost invariably selected for their ability as teachers. No attempt was made to cross-examine candidates, or even ask a few basic questions about resource or manpower management. I found that applicants had not the slightest idea of what a school cost to run, and there was, frankly, no reason why they should.

It was not relevant, at least up until this time. Even if they were interested, their employers could not produce the facts. In any case, it was thought not to be relevant to the professional management of teaching. Another thing which surprised me was that, when asked this question, very few people were able to make an intelligent guess, even though they must have known the size of the school they were applying to work in: most certainly they should have had an idea of the national figure for unit pupil costs. In other words, the efficient management of the school was not considered relevant to the efficient delivery of teaching.

Many would say that this is all very well, but schools are very different from commercial concerns. They are not in the business to make a profit, but to teach children, two totally different concepts. This is correct, but I would claim that to achieve the most effective teaching there must be proper management of people and financial resources, as well as of the curriculum, and this must be done as far as possible within the school. In other words, although the objectives of a school and a commercial firm are totally different, the tools they use to achieve the best results are the same.

Another fundamental problem in the beginning was to convince the educational world at large, or at least in sufficient numbers, of the need to get the pilot scheme off the ground. This problem resolved itself with the inclusion of Tyrrell Burgess, of the North East London Polytechnic, in the steering group. He came to talk about educational finance to the PTA at Comberton Village College at a critical moment, and I happened to go to this meeting. Tyrrell Burgess is very well known for the advice that he has given and is giving in this area and throughout many countries. It seemed to me that he would be an admirable person to involve in this scheme from its inception. He would be a professional advisor from outside the authority, and would give the Pilot Scheme respectability in the eyes of the educational world. His presence has been invaluable. He has been with us from the start and understands all the problems that a democratic organisation has to cope with, the complexity of the distribution of resources, and the requirements of the teaching profession. On many occasions during our discussions, Tyrrell Burgess has, in a few brief comments, been able to offer a more objective view of what we are discussing, and bring us back to the realities of life! At the same time, I think that he has gone a long way to convince the educational world of what we are trying to do, and that it is worthwhile.

Other people from outside have also joined us. Dr Joan Williamson from the Open University was seconded to us for a time to report back on what we were doing. She also carried out some research on the impact of the scheme on the schools concerned, looking at it from the school's point of view. Being a teacher herself, she was able to give considerable reassurance to the staff in these schools, a very important contribution. We were also joined for a while by John Kennedy from the Audit Commission who was able to contribute yet another dimension to our discussions.

All this made us question the whole way we went about providing our administrative structure for the education service and for the schools and their Governing Bodies. This also raised questions over the way the area officers were going about their business. Many changes have had to be made, and I believe that, once the whole authority is operating on LFM, many more will have to be carried out. I believe that this alters the whole conception, or perhaps ethos, of area management. It becomes very much a question of monitoring and seeing that standards are maintained within the policies of the LEA, rather than implementing.

Another invaluable by-product was the emphasis given to the partnership between teachers, finance officers, education officers, and councillors. We were all well aware in the past that there could be very little understanding and cooperation among these groups. This meant that essential cooperation was often sadly lacking in the education service. In fact, I believe, finance officers were viewed with a deep suspicion, and often seen as tools for making cuts in the provision at the chalk face. This was at a time when senior education managers were not given the management information that was required to operate the service, and when outside pressures made more and more restrictions on the resources available. This in itself created quite unacceptable pressures on a few senior officers.

The arrival of LFM in the pilot schools changed the whole climate of the relationship, and created a cooperative team to face up to the common problems, rather than opposing factions trying to defend their respective corners. LFM also immediately posed the question of how both staff and governors should be involved.

The impact on governors

In my own school, which has an exceptionally large Governing Body of 38, the introduction of LFM concentrated the governors' minds on the best way of going about their business in general. There had been concern for some considerable time that the Governing Body was becoming progressively more ineffective, as it attempted to take on ever-growing responsibilities, with some governors wishing and needing to know more about the running of their school. Governors' meetings could take up to four hours and the situation was quite obviously becoming unworkable.

With the arrival of LFM, it became imperative to set up a special sub-committee of governors who had a particular interest in management and resources. To achieve this it was necessary to divide up the full Governing Body into several sub-committees so that all governors had the opportunity of looking in detail at various aspects of the school's activities. The LFM sub-committee went into the accounts' details with a fine tooth comb, and found, in these early days, that the information provided by Shire Hall was riddled with discrepancies. An immense amount of work was required to get the information sorted out and, perhaps more significantly, understood. As the figures were clarified, we were able to investigate various problems, such as why the ancillary cost for cleaners seemed to be more than we could possibly pay out in a year. The investigation revealed that a number of the primary school costs were being charged to the Village College. Such painstaking work took time and effort, but it indicated the kind of thing that would be exposed when the new accounts system was brought into use and the details investigated at local level.

The result of all this was that we set up a proper structure for sub-committees within the Governing Body (which we should have done long ago) such as a finance sub-committee (which was the specialist LFM sub-committee), personnel sub-committee, curriculum sub-committee and a grounds and building sub-committee, together with one or two working parties. All sub-committees had executive powers for day to day matters. This meant that things were examined in more detail by interested governors, who could sit on two sub-committees if they chose. Also, teaching staff were involved as co-opted members in various sub-committees, over and above the official staff governors, which greatly helped to increase communication and consultation.

The early LFM committee included three members of staff as co-opted members. Although they did not have any vote, they provided invaluable information, and over the course of time an ever-growing detailed input. But I think the most important thing of all was the general improvement in communications at a personal level. This went a very great way to easing the underlying hostility that the scheme was creating in some quarters, and was the answer to the fundamental difficulty of having real consultations in a practical way. We now have staff members who, though not necessarily in favour of all, or even any, aspects of the scheme, at least understand the parameters of the problem, and what we were driving at, and can now explain what the system is about.

Bridging the LEA – school gap

One of the great difficulties with the scheme, as said earlier, was the fundamental problem of governors and staff understanding that managers still have to manage, while they set the policies and direction, and saw to it that they were achieved. In just the same way, council members were having difficulty in devolving responsibility for operations while still maintaining overall control. Initially, I think, quite a number of governors and staff members had difficulty in accepting responsibility for the wider powers that they now had. There was also a further, rather amusing by-product: for years we, the Elected Councillors, had been criticised by people in the schools who said that headquarters did not really know what was wanted, and they knew far better themselves. But when schools were given the power to make more of their own decisions, the same people thought that in some way the local managers would be abusing the opportunity that they had been given! They seemed to have difficulty in accepting that the motivation of professional people in the schools was going to be in the best interest of the establishment. Perhaps this could occur on rare occasions, but the risk is far outweighed by the advantages of having local decisions, and of course it does also emphasise the need for overall monitoring.

Many advantages became apparent at an early stage, which are not perhaps directly relevant to the accounts. It was the first time, in my knowledge, that different groups such as governors, staff, heads, education officers and finance officers – all of whom had got interests in the success of education – worked closely together.

In the beginning there was a vast difference of opinion as to where we were going and what we were trying to do, and even the understanding of the fundamental concepts was a problem. But as time wore on, it was surprising how a consensus grew up, and this was an immense help in getting the scheme together and alive. As I said right at the beginning, we had to start practising to find out what we were able to achieve.

Information systems

One of the biggest problems that we had, and still have, is that of inaccuracies in the detailed accounts. These showed up as the County Council macro budget accounts were broken down to establishments. Mistakes and miscodings which had been occurring in the past, were exposed and had to be put right; getting things coded correctly in the first place is not easy and requires considerable discipline in the schools.

As governors and staff began to gain experience and confidence, more and more details were required, with a bigger breakdown of management information. At times, people tended to lose their sense of perspective, and get very concerned about the minor discrepancies, that in percentage terms had little or no effect upon the operation of the total budget; when one considered the way that the school budget was arrived at in the first place, these details were almost irrelevant. Unfortunately there are severe limitations on the accounting process being operated in the county at the moment, but now that we understand more clearly what we want, establishments will have to have a larger and more detailed breakdown of management information than we have been capable of producing in the past.

In Autumn 1987 we were operating on the county computer which was programmed in the 70s to provide accounting information for the macro budget of the County Council. This is excellent, as far as it goes, but we are now asking the programme for management information which it was not originally designed to provide. The LFM schools can now say what kind of breakdown they require, and obviously this can be programmed into a macro budget system but to do this the complete accountancy position has to be reprogrammed. In any case, this is becoming overdue. It obviously takes time and considerable expense but it will have to be done in the next three years. I must say, in passing, that it is quite clear that an LFM scheme cannot work if the central computer cannot produce the detailed management information for the schools, and also the monitoring information required to control the whole system, to ensure that the members have an overall policy control.

The 'academic plan'

Perhaps we should now consider another aspect, to which I do not think very much thought had been given at the initial stage. The forward plan for the school, known as the academic plan, details numbers of pupils, subjects, and necessary staff over the next few years. This, in turn, dictates the teacher requirements, as the number of pupils per class, the number of classes required, and when they will be required. The governors can thus see the number of teachers required to produce the curriculum they wish to have, which may well be out of step with the resources that they are going to be allowed. The plan, therefore, gives the governors the opportunity to look into the future and thus to make staffing decisions for the present, which will fit in with the staffing decisions they are going to have to make in the next two or three years. A proper debate can take place, with the interested people, on reduction or expansion of staff, well in advance of decisions which have to be taken, so that we can get the optimum result from limited resources. Incidentally, this could, if operated properly, considerably affect the decision-making process for members of the education authority. They would be properly informed of the basic problems of the service at the resource planning stage, as it means that detailed problems can be exposed on the macro scale, and specific steps can be taken to meet this. Also, it is only practicable to get extra resources in year three of the County Council's medium term plan. The plan means that proper lobbying can be made on the three-year time scale, which will greatly assist the management of the service as a whole.

Formula budgeting

This brings me to the vexed question of formula budgeting. Again, it was quite clear when investigating unit costs in various schools, that there were differences between one school and another which could not be explained by a number of known differences. In other words, the historical build-up of the existing budgets for schools was unfair, with variations between one educational area and another, and between one school and another. In saying this, I am not offering criticism on past decisions as, quite frankly, there was neither the management structure, the information, nor the will to see to it that there was a totally fair distribution of resources. Could the money be divided up more fairly, more logically? Certainly the current system was far from logical. We thought it could be. After all, the main cost element in a school is the pupil, and it ought to be possible to produce a formula whose main element should be based on pupil numbers, with various factors for the special cases.

Also, it appeared obvious from an early stage that the central finance team could not handle the individual historical budgets for all establishments without a vast increase in staff, and in any case, it was doubtful whether this would serve a useful purpose. The abolition of a historical budget meant the abolition of hundreds of questions, mostly irrelevant, with governing bodies challenging their budget for each heading line by line. Basically, we wanted a system which was understandable to staff and governing bodies, and could be looked at with some confidence over the next two or three years as an indication of the way their budget would be going. Obviously with a recognisable and relatively simple formula, governing bodies can work out their income against their academic plan, and plan accordingly. The County Council could well top up, or cut back, the totality of the money from one year to the next, but the County Council itself has a three year medium-term plan so it is possible to predict, with a fair degree of certainty, the resources available for three years. I believe that this gives the stability to schools to make really serious management planning decisions for the future.

Arriving at a formula is not easy as there are bound to be gains and losses. We have looked at dozens of formulae but all in all the pattern is remarkably similar between one approach and another. Even if you measure the differences in prospective formulae, they pale into insignificance when compared with some of the differences between the current historical budgets. This formula needs to reflect, as near as is possible, the historical budgets, having taken out the worst discrepancies. It is inevitable that some schools will gain and other schools will lose. It will be for councillors, in due course, to decide where these changes occur, although the impact can be cushioned over two or three years. Considerable passion is raised over this, with everybody forgetting that they are arguing about a very small part of their total budget, a part probably within the unexplained variations between historical budgets.

I believe that this formula can be made to work, and to meet the number of special requirements which will affect some schools but not others. Where there are losses, I believe that the general benefits of LFM, once the situation has stabilised, will offset a small loss of resources in some establishments. There are, however, one or two very special cases to which further thought has to be given.

Conclusion

To sum up, efficient management in our schools is absolutely essential for the wellbeing of the education authority as a whole, and the quality of education of its pupils. I believe that LFM is the tool with which to achieve this. As a result of implementing LFM we would have:

1.   better governors;
2.   better governor – staff relationships;
3.   formula distribution of finance, with a limit to eradicate unfairness;
4.   more sensitive decisions, made locally;
5.   more consultation on what is being delivered and by whom;
6.   the ability for governing bodies to have involved discussions with the authority to improve future budgets;
7.   the ability to concentrate councillors' minds on what *needs* to be done rather than on *how* it should be done.
8.   the ability to plan ahead with confidence.

Questions for discussion

1 *Robert James sees LFM as having been the catalyst for necessary structural changes within the Governing Body. What changes would need to be made in the procedures of the Governing Bodies with which you are familiar, for LFM to be implemented successfully?*

2 *Do you agree with Robert James's view that too many councillors get over-involved in the minutiae of decision-making? What experiences lead you to hold your opinions?*

3 *Do you think that what Robert James describes as the 'deep-end treatment' is the only way in which a major organisational change can be brought about in the educational world? If you disagree, what would be your preferred way of introducing an LFM scheme?*

4 *Robert James raises (page 50) the question of the management qualifications of candidates for headteacher posts. Do you think selection procedures may change in future in the light of LFM? As a practical exercise, the group might plan how the headship selection for a secondary school should take place in future. As a simulation, members of the group could act as candidates while the others are the interviewing panel.*

5 *What is the evidence in this chapter that many of the early decisions and strategies in the Cambridgeshire scheme were based on 'acts of faith', hunches and 'conviction politics'?* •

6 *Robert James suggests that there is a clash of interests in councillors between being 'managers' and 'people committed to looking after the best interests of their own electoral division'. Can you think of examples where this clash of interest might occur? Do you agree that LFM can only thrive in a political climate where there is a clear overall majority held by one party (so that electoral problems are minimised)?*

Chapter 3 LFM in a primary school
Audrey Stenner

As head of the only primary school in the 1982 pilot scheme, Audrey Stenner gives a positive but balanced picture of what LFM has meant to her school and how it has affected the governors, the teaching and non-teaching staff, the pupils and herself. She stresses that LFM is only a means to an end and expresses some controversial views about the positive aspects of being a small school in an LFM system.

There is a hardy sentiment, though no hard evidence to support it, that primary schools are essentially different from secondary schools and therefore different treatment is appropriate for them. It came as no surprise, then, that Cambridgeshire's initial proposal to delegate financial responsibility related to the secondary sector only. However, it seemed to the governors and head of Buckden, a village primary school with 350 on roll, that if devolution were to be as beneficial to schools as was being suggested, it would be a pity not to extend those benefits to primary schools as well. At the least, it merited a trial to find out whether LFM could work successfully in a primary school. They were encouraged in their belief in the potential of local management by Buckden's experience of the Increased Financial Responsibility Scheme (IFRS), the precursor to LFM. IFRS had originated in the Huntingdon administrative area of the county in 1977 and had offered to those primary heads who wanted to take it, their first opportunity of having wider financial responsiblity than was open to them within the restricted sphere of the capitation allowance.

The scope of IFRS was limited but under it Buckden had made modest profits and had seen the advantages of being able to use money saved on the telephone account, for instance, to provide more books and resources. There is a definite incentive to a school to manage its costs efficiently, in accordance with its own needs and priorities, when there is an element of reward for good management. Not only was the ability to shift funds from one heading to another advantageous but the enablement to carry credits on to the following year allowed some pre-planning and avoided that unsatisfactory end-of-year scramble to spend up exactly. The possibility of managing a much more comprehensive budget than under IFRS therefore seemed an attractive one.

Another factor in Buckden's interest in taking part in LFM was a feeling of frustration at being unable to direct funds to where, in the school's judgement, they were most needed. One example had occurred some two or three years previously when draught excluders were fitted to all the outer doors. They were neither needed nor requested (moreover after the work was completed the infants could no longer open the doors unaided) but at the same time requests for urgently needed furniture were being turned down 'because there was no money'. To the authority the outlay represented assumed savings on fuel but to the school the real necessity at the time was enough chairs to seat the children.

Some fairly sustained lobbying about primary participation was required and the outlook did not seem promising. No one was more surprised than the head of Buckden, who was a co-opted member of the Education Committee, when her amendment to that effect was passed. Members decided that two primary schools should take part in the pilot scheme, a city school and Buckden. The city school soon withdrew, for reasons which were not disclosed, and thus the pilot group emerged as six secondary schools and one primary. The chief concerns expressed by some members and representatives of the teachers' organisations at that time were doubts about whether primary schools were suitable for self-management, whether primary heads could cope with the increased work-load and whether, in any case, they had better uses for their time than controlling a budget. Several members expressed their surprise and real concern that a primary school should want to look after its own finance 'because it is such a big responsiblity and the officers can do the job for you'. This remark revealed the well-intentioned protectiveness shown towards primary schools, which sits strangely alongside the enormous degree of trust and independence given to them in curriculum matters.

The misgivings were shared by a number of heads, who were reluctant to extend their role. They came into the profession, they said, to teach, not to do a glorified accounts job. They had no wish to become financial managers because it was not a role appropriate to the position of a headteacher. There were other primary heads who were eager, then and later, to enter the pilot scheme. They saw no dichotomy between the educational and managerial functions of the Head because in reality these interlocked. They believed that they would be better managers of education if they also managed the resources. In the event there were to be no more primary participants in LFM until four years later, despite Buckden's attempts to get some more included.

One of the obstacles for primary schools is administrative, in that there is a global budget for them, while secondary schools have their own. LFM involved constructing an individual budget for a primary school for the first time. While Buckden awaited its first budget the head asked all the governors and teachers to estimate the annual running costs of the school. No one knew what they were since it was information which it had not hitherto been thought necessary for schools to know and the estimates ranged from £20,000 to £2 million. When the budget came it totalled £165,450 and had been built up as follows:

	£
Employees	
Teachers	130 940
Supply cover	580
Ancillary	7370
Caretaker and cleaners	7730
Premises	
Fuel, light, heating	6790
Furniture and fittings	260
Rent and rates	7730
Supplies and services	
Office purchases	30
Cleaning equipment	80
Capitation	3660
Laundry	20
Transport	
Mileage allowance	150
Establishment expenses	
Postage	90
Printing and stationery	110
Staff advertising	20
Telephone	550
Income	
Rent and lettings	660
TOTAL	165 450

The time-scale was such that there was very little time for preparation or training and in any case there was almost no experience in other LEAs on which to draw. Solihull's scheme (1981) had pre-dated LFM but it had started with the explicit intention that the authority should share in any financial benefits which came through increased efficiency. Cambridgeshire, however, saw the transfer of savings as a strong disincentive to initiatives at school level and constructed its own framework for devolution. In the absence of detailed information it seemed to the teachers at Buckden that participation in LFM would in large measure be an act of faith. In the series of meetings which was held the head could provide few facts and no guarantees at all. They were a hard-working and dedicated group of teachers who saw their function as 'getting the children on' and the burden of their questioning concerned how much work LFM would mean for class teachers. In summary, staff opinion was that they all wanted to decide priorities and share in policy-making but they did not want a lot of financial detail to come their way. Additional concerns were whether the school would lose money in the following year if it had made a profit and whether it would start off with a budget which was 'right'.

The long discussions were most useful in clarifying for everyone what their expectations were and how perceptions concerning accountability varied. Some believed that teachers *should* be accountable for the school's expenditure, but to parents, not to the LEA; some felt responsible but not accountable to parents; some believed that they were directly accountable to the CEO; and others saw themselves as accountable in the first instance to the head and their colleagues. There was unanimity on three issues: the classroom came first; a definite assurance was wanted that the scheme would not lead to a cut-back in next year's allocation; there was no real opposition to LFM, though there were some doubts.

LFM does not alter the aims of education, it is concerned with ways and means, so the first requirement at Buckden was to set some objectives for local management. These were:

- to create better learning opportunities;
- to involve all the governors and staff in decision-making;
- to make LFM relevant to the curriculum;
- to use the flexibility of LFM to get the most out of the resources available;
- to show the costs of a primary school;
- to monitor progress and to watch for adverse effects.

The school did not 'plan for' conflict; no policy was formulated at this stage to cope with dispute between the governors, head and teachers. That came later, not because dissension occurred, but because the area inspector advised that agreed procedures ought to be in existence beforehand. To date there has been no occasion to use them.

On entry to the scheme the chairman of governors had delegated all LFM matters to the vice-chairman who set up a small sub-committee of governors and teachers. But in practice most of the business in the first year was done in staff meetings and through the vice-chairman, because few decisions were taken. It was instead a time for learning, since there was no means of knowing whether the budget would be adequate. The supply heading, to take one item, looked disturbingly low and it was thought imprudent to make major changes which would have cost implications for subsequent years, before the annual pattern of expenditure had become apparent. One point about LFM is that, while it gives a school the freedom to make decisions, it does not force it to make any, if it chooses not to do so.

Progress was regularly reviewed at staff and governor meetings and by the end of the first year both knowledge and confidence had substantially increased. Although the financial outcomes were negligible – the school was in credit by just £700 – the intangible gains were reckoned to be far more significant. For example, the ability to respond quickly to a situation without having to wait for a decision from the Area Office was particularly useful in the case of absence. Among other benefits, it was felt that working together on something new and problematic had promoted a stronger sense of professional identity and corporate responsibility.

That is not to say that the first year was not an anxious and even daunting one at times. There was no shortage of people saying that a primary school was not suitable for financial management and that Buckden would be bankrupt. Moreover, LFM sometimes seemed like a financial minefield; the more probing was done, the more anomalies were revealed and unknown facts uncovered, for it was new ground for the officers as well as for the schools. The Review and Evaluation Group meetings provided excellent on-the-job training as councillors, officers, chairmen and heads engaged together in finding solutions to problems.

The head had undertaken all LFM administration by choice in order to gain experience and has continued to do it, although the secretary prepares the employee costs when the budget is being built up. The workload is not onerous and time spent on LFM averages out at about one and a half hours a week over the school year. At budget preparation time more hours are needed but in other weeks none at all. More time-consuming than administration is attendance at LFM meetings and visits from people interested in the scheme. The Cambridgeshire division of the National Union of Teachers (1986) has criticised what it saw as the LEA's inadequate analysis of the training requirements for LFM heads, but in the opinion of the writer, who has no accountancy skills and dislikes figures, the difficulties have been exaggerated. There were skills to be learned but they were not complex and are well within the competency of the ordinary head. Certainly for a primary school budget a simple paper system and some commonsense are found to be enough.

Financial prospects for the second year looked considerably brighter because more realistic estimates had been achieved by negotiation, notably on supply and fuel. When Cambridgeshire introduced privatised cleaning, the school opted to tender for its own cleaning contract, an arrangement which pleased the cleaning staff because above all it allowed flexibility. The caretaker was able to buy extra cleaning hours out of the budget, keep his known and loyal cleaners and arrange their hours as it suited. For the school it was an advantage to have another group of people brought within the orbit of LFM and working to a common aim. Enthusiasm was the keynote of the second year, both in the school and in the Review Group meetings, which were characterised by the very buoyant attitudes of the various partners. There was a heady sense of 'frontiership' with entrepreneurial ideas in plenty being floated: capital loans, privatisation of refuse collection, renting school premises to banks/building societies, school cheque book administration and selling off assets such as excess play-ing-field acreage. The last two were rejected. The urge to exploit the potential of the scheme was most evident, and perhaps startling to some councillors. At the same time the degree of virement being exer-cised by the schools, around 2%, seemed surprisingly low to observers.

Buckden's savings in that year were £9200, of which approximately half were planned and half adventitious. The planned part came from an accumulation of underspends on supply, electricity, oil, telephone, water and others. Economies were achieved by such means as using cheap telephone time, pupil post, arrangements for evening classes which did not involve heating the entire school for one flower club, installing gadgets in the urinals which saved hundreds of gallons of metered water during weekends and holidays, and more thoughtful use of electricity. The supply underspend was generated by the head and a part-time teacher covering for absence whenever possible, a direct saving to the school of £50 a day. In addition three teachers at the top of the scale had left for promotion and three younger ones came on a lower salary point. It has never been the governors' policy to appoint 'cheap' teachers and in some years the staffing budget has been overspent, while in others there have been fortuitous savings. A small point on nomenclature is perhaps appropriate here. At Buckden 'carry-forward', 'profits', 'underspend', and 'savings', were used synonymously but it was noticeable that, to critics of the scheme at least, 'underspend' was the most acceptable term, perhaps because it is less suggestive of commercialism than 'profits' and less indicative of frugality than 'savings'. In this year Buckden's underspend was the highest among the seven schools in percentage terms (5.2%). Among the secondary schools the average LFM underspend was 2.3% compared with the non-LFM average of 0.1%.

The staff had meetings to decide how to allocate the underspend and then put their proposals to the governors for approval:

	£
Restocking class fiction libraries	1500
Computer equipment	900
Mathematics resources	300
Audio-visual equipment	800
Playground equipment	500
Furniture	1500
Extra cleaning hours	50
In-service training	350
Supply teacher to release staff for training	800
Start to office computerisation	1000
Contingency fund	2000
	9200

Since 1983 the school has simply been allocated a gross sum, from which it has made up its own budget. The procedures for deciding priorities for next year's budget and for allotting any underspend were improved after the second year by having joint meetings for all the governors and staff to make the decisions together. The model of decision-making which has evolved is partly collegial and partly based on a 'market-system', in that individual teachers and governors put in bids for sums of money. They have to convince the others that the bid is sound for reasons of development, current deficiencies, or whatever it might be, and then a decision is made by everyone about priority order or, if ideas race ahead of resources, which projects are to be deferred.

At Buckden the use of the budget as a planning instrument could be better developed. Ideally all decisions about virement should be part of the forward planning but a combination of early caution and the timing of the receipt of the final accounts (late in the summer term) had produced a bias towards a save-then-spend pattern, retrospective virement, as it were. The 1986/7 budget, however, was constructed as a quantitative statement of a plan of action beause it was felt to be important to test the school's needs-related estimates against the county's incremental allocation. Whereas in previous years the school had adjusted its requirements to the given allowance, it was now saying: 'This is what we believe needs to be spent at Buckden. We want to establish adequate levels of ancillary and clerical help; we propose a programme of in-service training which will cost money; we know that some non-contact time would be beneficial for primary teachers'. Needless to say, this budget overshot the county's allowance – by £3300 – and, also not unexpectedly, it had to be paid back in the following year, but it was nevertheless a most useful exercise for those who worked in the school and knew its needs to construct a zero-based budget.

In the year 1987/8 Buckden is taking part in another trial run by the LEA, this time with formula distribution. The gain, on the criteria currently adopted, is about £1600 over the traditional budget. There is much officer work to be done before an equitable formula can be designed for primary schools of different size. Buckden's budget in this, the sixth year of LFM, is £206 000.

Local management quickly established itself as a routine way of life at Buckden; people were not self-conscious about it nor did they go about with a banner of LFM before their eyes. An evaluation at the end of the pilot scheme showed that governors and staff believed that it had had significant value in bringing considerable educational, financial, social and organisational benefits to the school. While it would be rash to claim that improved reading averages and the like can be attributed necessarily to LFM, it has most certainly created better conditions for learning. At the most basic level children no longer have to share a maths textbook between three and the school is better resourced than it has ever been. It has turned savings made under non-educational headings into books, computers, instruments, equipment, furniture and it wants for very little of that nature. The teachers can make curriculum decisions in the knowledge, not just the hope, that they can be resourced and extra teaching and ancillary hours are financed each year.

In financial terms the benefits are unarguable. Buckden has done well out of LFM and average savings of around £9000 a year have been a substantial asset to it. Other financial effects, though less self-evident, are important too. For example the governors and staff have a greatly increased knowledge and awareness of finance at school and LEA level. They have learned a great deal about how and why schools are financed in the way they are; although they may not always agree with the principles they at least know what they are and the whole process seems less arbitrary. They can now give well-informed answers to parents too. Everyone has become confident, through experience, about taking responsibility for public money and those involved feel self-reliant and enterprising about taking on other costs such as catering, maintenance and transport. There is also an incentive to make the premises and facilities work for the school when it can keep the lettings income. 'Value for money' is an imprecise term, but whatever people understand by it, that is what they feel they are aiming for and achieving. Furthermore it saves administrative time not to have to whittle the last penny out of the capitation allowance and a measure of financial independence frees the school from the need to adopt the suppliant position. It is not obliged to rely on parental fund-raising to the same degree and teachers can put their time and initiative to better professional use than organising jumble sales.

It would be misleading to imply that the only benefits open to a school through LFM are those for which it pays. The organisational and social changes for which LFM was the catalyst at Buckden are many and include a style of collaborative decision-making which is a pledge by everyone that they have a responsibility for the school as a whole, a sort of directorship. Local management can promote greater coherence in classrooms as well as in council chambers. LFM also offers plenty of scope for practical management training and career teachers like the deputy head have found their job satisfaction enhanced by it. All the governors and staff were brought together in a working relationship for the first time and there was much social value in learning together. Contact between the groups increased and from that came better understanding by the one of the functions and aspirations of the other, as well as a closer association between the governors and the PTA. LFM offers a much more dynamic role in governorship to those who want it.

The children also play their part and take some pride in it. If expressed in simple terms, local financial responsibility is understandable by junior children and it is beneficial if they see that they too can contribute. A request not to squander paper towels has a distant appeal in itself but when it is linked to desirable consequences in tangible form it immediately has some meaning. Such few accounts as there are of school-based finance completely ignore the role of pupils, as if efficiency were a paper exercise solely for senior managers, but that is to overlook the social advantages of everyone sharing in the betterment of their environment. As incentives are offered through

LFM from the LEA to the school so they are passed on within it and the chidren are consulted about their preferences for some of the savings. One outcome, naturally enough, has been some splendid additions to the playground equipment.

There were also costs associated with bringing LFM into the school. These related almost entirely to the time given to it in the first year. Everyone gave extra hours to discussing, learning about and reviewing the scheme and at that time no one knew whether it would be time well spent. As one teacher said later: 'Once the benefits began to appear it all seemed worthwhile. The time was well invested because LFM is the best thing which has happened to this school'. It is a view shared by governors, teachers and head.

During the third year of the pilot the head had asked the county's primary inspectors to make an appraisal of LFM at Buckden. It seemed reasonable to expect that a school should operate with some degree of certainty about what were the educational outcomes of an innovation, and appropriate therefore to try to identify whether or not local management had an effect on children's learning. On two counts it was no easy assignment for the inspectors: first, they had not been involved with LFM; second, it is extremely difficult, if not impossible, to quantify the relationship between financial input and educational results. The inspectors spent three days in the school and three reports followed: the main document, a synopsis for general circulation and a confidential report for the school. The inspectors made certain recommendations, the most important of which, in terms of the development of primary LFM, was that an extended pilot scheme should be undertaken using a random sample of conscripted schools, the better to evaluate the advantages and disadvantages of LFM. Because of Buckden's relatively large size its experience was reckoned to be no certain indicator of the viability of LFM in primary schools, indeed the inspectors specifically recommended that LFM should not be considered appropriate in schools where the head had a 50% or greater teaching commitment.

When the extended scheme got underway in 1986 it included some very small schools with just such teaching heads. Eleven schools in all are currently engaged in the three-year project and it is expected that the County Council will make a decision about LFM in primary schools in 1989. Almost all the pilot schools are positive about their experience of local management. At the end of the first year all were in credit and some had made substantial savings.

It is unfortunate therefore that the Secretary of State for Education, Kenneth Baker, should be limiting his otherwise laudable proposals for financial devolution, to schools of not less than 200 pupils (although LEAs may be given the option to include smaller ones). On what criteria the cut-off was decided is not apparent but there was, and is, no evidence that schools below 200 cannot manage their own finances. It would seem more objective if such schools were to be given the chance to judge for themselves whether a measure of autonomy which did not exist before is worthwhile to them, since only they can know whether the opportunity costs, such as the alternative use of time, are too great. LFM is part of a long-term trend, now accelerating, towards giving greater freedom to teachers and governors to manage their own institutions; would-be LFM schools might well question the moral and educational implications of some schools possessing a right to take decisions which others may never have, because they have been deemed to be too small. Grading schools by suitability of size is administratively appealing but it is also divisive. Mr Baker's plan may serve to accentuate divisions which already exist.

Clearly there is more flexibility in a budget of £1.7 million than in one of £70,000 and in that respect LFM favours large schools, but it is all too easy to attach too much importance to financial results and to lose sight of the fact that budgetary control is an instrument, not an end in itself. The potential benefits of local management to primary schools are by no means confined to the end-of-year balance. Even were savings to be marginal or non-existent, the ability to make financial decisions in the light of local knowledge is a most significant step forward for primary schools and one which should lead to expenditure being more closely matched to their real needs.

It has, nevertheless, to be acknowledged that there are difficulties about the generalisation of LFM. The primary part of the national education system consists of thousands of schools of varying size. Some of them are very small, many of them have teaching heads, and all of them have a poor level of clerical support, relative to secondary schools. Accommodating LFM to a system of such scale and diversity poses considerable administrative problems because devolution, initially, makes for more complexities in a system. On that ground it is understandable that assumptions about suitability-by-size-of-school might quickly be made. On the other hand, it could be argued that perceived disadvantages are evidence of the need to change the system rather than of the inappropriateness of local management. The existence of teaching heads, arguably, is a questionable matter in itself and every school should be able to count on sufficient clerical help. Cambridgeshire's extended pilot scheme may draw necessary attention to the needs of the smallest schools and thereby benefit all of them in the long term.

Since much of the case against primary schools rests upon the supposed handicap of their size it is easy to overlook the fact that there may be benefit in that size for the operation of LFM. There are some areas where smallness could be said to be an advantage. First, in a small school it is easier to involve all the staff and governors in decision making. It is not necessary to have sub-committees (which may seem divisive to those who do not sit on them) because all the interested parties can attend the same meeting. The probability of genuine consultation ought to be higher in such a situation and union fears of the non-involvement of teachers less likely to be realised. Second, the network of relationships is simpler and conversation with individual teachers a more usual way of communicating than notices in the staffroom or a mailing-list. Communication is not just a matter of passing information or decisions downwards; the upward flow of information, essential for successful management, is likely to be more efficient when personal contact is more frequent. Third, the likelihood is that staff can more easily establish common goals when they work at close quarters in one building and when departmental structures are a less dominant feature of the organisation. In these circumstances small schools may well develop a style of local management from which large ones could usefully draw lessons.

A further case for extending financial control is the serious lack of available data about the costs of individual primary schools. Referring to this neglected area of study as a 'dark continent', Knight (1983) observed:

We know much less about the cost structure of primary schools in England than we do about those in Nigeria or Indonesia. We know really very little indeed about how and why costs vary between different types and sizes of primary schools and how they can be altered and influenced . . . We know less about their costs than we know about the costs of our fish-and-chip shops'.

(*Managing School Finance* p 90)

The more financial information is forthcoming from single primary schools, the greater is the possibility that attention will turn to the imbalances between the funding of the different sectors and that one day they will be adjusted more in favour of the primary field. The differences are sharply evident when budgets are examined in detail side by side as they were during the pilot scheme. Capitation allowances too might usefully come under scrutiny – there appears to be no good reason why they should continue in their present form unchallenged. The reliance on historical budgeting surely has to stop at some time and one might surmise that the disparity between secondary and primary resourcing will, sometime in the future, seem as unreasonable a tradition as was that of having different salary scales for men and women teachers before 1961.

The Education Select Committee's report *Achievement in Primary*

Schools (1986) pointed out that the differential resourcing of primary and secondary schools was one aspect of an entrenched and misguided tradition and it stressed the primary sector's entitlement to better funding. If global budgeting were to become a thing of the past there is every chance that the inequalities in the system would be highlighted. The capitation allowances in Cambridgeshire for 1987/8 are:

Primary pupils aged 5–11	£24
Secondary pupils aged 11–16	£56
aged 16+	£102

Looking to the future, it will be fascinating to watch the development of schemes like LFM in primary schools across the country if Mr Baker's plans go ahead – and there seems to be every indication that they will. The prospect raises a number of interesting issues. Will primary teachers see financial delegation as an enfranchisement or as an imposition? Will they interpret the conveyancing of local management to them as a welcome manifestation of political confidence in their professional capabilities, a confidence which they may feel has not been much in evidence during the recent period of strained relationships between Whitehall and the teachers' organisations? What will be the effect of widescale devolution on the number and quality of recruits to primary governorship? How will their articles of government, which do not refer to financial rights or duties, be amended? Some heads and governors may feel it necessary that their financial accountabilities be defined separately and precisely if ill-contrived schemes are hastily pushed through. What is not yet clear in central government policy statements is whether it is also proposed to develop instruments which would give parents, *qua* parents, the right to intervene directly in financial decision-making. Some recent proposals in Scotland suggest that local management might take that direction. A further question is whether experience of financial management would be a prerequisite before primary schools were given permission to opt out of local authority control.

It would be premature to conjecture too far ahead on the possible nature and consequences of decentralising schemes. Financial management is but a recent initiative for primary schools and it is impossible to predict with certainty how it will develop. What can be said is that Cambridgeshire's scheme is probably the portent of radical changes in the way primary education has traditionally been managed.

Questions for discussion

1   *What aspects of Audrey Stenner's experience might give the greatest reassurance to an unconvinced primary head?*

2   *Do you agree with her assertion that to prevent people from experiencing LFM, on grounds of size, with an inevitably arbitrary cut-off point, is likely to be divisive and demoralising?*

3   *Do you agree with Audrey Stenner's view that LFM will make more people become 'militant' about the disparity of capitation funding between a 10+ child in a primary school and an 11+ child in a secondary school? Can you justify or explain the figures quoted on page 72 for Cambridgeshire?*

4   *At the end of her article (page 72), Audrey Stenner raises a number of questions about how primary schools might be expected to react to LFM. In your view, which one is likely to raise the most serious worries and how would you set out to calm these worries?*

5   *Here are some comments made by primary heads at the end of the first year of the extended primary pilot scheme:*

'One year is too soon to be making assessments.'

'I found it difficult at first to see where all the budget figures came from as they seemed to bear little relationship to spending patterns.'

'The "turnover factor" is a nonsense when applied to a small school when nobody leaves.'

'The school is a better school for being in the LFM pilot. It is a more efficient unit which is better resourced than would otherwise have been the case and the children benefit directly.'

'Time spent on the management of LFM is now minimal – a couple of hours a month.'

'I enjoy the feeling that I have some control and say in my school's budget. I have been more careful and understand more about school costs. I like the idea that, as a staff, we can say what our needs are when we have spare money.'

'I was very "anti" to begin with but now I am a convert.'

'If LFM becomes accepted policy, will small schools get the opportunity of opting in if they want to?'

Which of these comments do you find surprising and why?

6   *Simulate a meeting at a primary school to discuss how you would use a carried-forward underspend of £9000. Share out the roles in the group: head, deputy head, teacher, chair of governors, teacher governor, parent governor, member of non-teaching staff.*

Chapter 4 LFM in a secondary school

George Thomas

George Thomas shows in detail what LFM has meant to him and the school of which he is head. He shows how the LFM scheme has affected the management structure within the school, creating problems as well as improvements. He highlights the positive contribution of governors and illustrates the range of optional solutions that can be considered when creating the budget. He affirms the need for better information systems but is quite explicit about the positive outcomes that have been achieved. He concludes by anticipating further extensions of the scope of LFM and welcomes formula budgeting as a way of distributing resources to schools.

An inauspicious beginning

Looking back to the beginning of the pilot scheme in Cambridgeshire, it is difficult to remember who actually initiated it. St Peter's School was already by-passing the Area Office in much of the payment of school accounts. This Increased Financial Responsibility (IFR), as it was called, entailed the school's accounts staff coding all invoices and despatching them direct to Shire Hall rather than to the Area Office. The discussions and ideas concerned with extending this scheme involved heads, officers and elected councillors at a time when Cambridgeshire was prepared to make radical changes. The paradox was that although the original Local Financial Management Scheme was, therefore, evolutionary in development, it was perceived as revolutionary. Furthermore, although considerable discussion took place, the detailed analysis of the Scheme was not communicated to the pilot schools until late February, 1982 – with the intention of introducing it in April. A full staff meeting was convened at St Peter's in order to outline the revised plans and to attempt to win support from the majority of staff, before putting the whole issue to the Governors.

The timing could not have been worse. Unions were just beginning to withdraw 'goodwill' in their attempts to support their negotiations for improved salaries and, therefore, two unions refused to attend any further meetings. Pressure groups were formed to support or oppose the implementation of the scheme. One union correspondent refused to allow her union members to attend meetings, but wrote to the Governing Body complaining that I had not consulted the staff. Staff expressed their fears to the Chief Education Officer that the scheme would give extraordinary powers to the head, yet those same people expressed fears to me that the scheme was allowing the education officers to abrogate their responsibilities of administering the school. Many staff voiced their concern that it was a covert means for councillors to reduce financial allocation to schools. They believed that staffing was safeguarded only by unions and the media, who forced the Council to agonise over staff cuts, with such effect that staff reductions were not taking place. A scheme by which money and not staff was allocated to schools seemed to let the Council off the 'agony' hook, and to place the onus of reducing staff upon the head and governors.

In St Peter's the introduction of the scheme was made possible, first by individual members of the Governing Body who saw themselves as radical in the true sense of the word in the changing nature of local government. Second, the area organiser of NUT spoke to his members in the school and persuaded them that we needed to be in the scheme in order to assess its viability. Third, I strongly believed that it would help the school and was determined to see it adopted.

Setting up a system

Although the title is Local Financial Management, it became difficult to divorce it from the widespread belief that it was really concerned with local financial *saving*. Perhaps this was inevitable: first because that was how individual staff perceived its aim, and second, because the financial year 1982–83 was used as a dry run, in which any planned savings would be retained by the school. From the start, therefore, we were determined to make savings to prove the success of the scheme. It has taken four years of consultation, amendment of views and practice to replace the savings concept by one of real proactive management. Even the most determined of us in 1982 saw it as a financial scheme to improve the resources of the school. What has happened is that it has revolutionised (and I use that word deliberately) the total management approach of the school. There was a very remarkable incident in one Board of Studies meeting, when in the middle of a discussion on finance, one head of department exclaimed that the dicussion was not financial at all but educational. That was the real breakthrough. From that moment finance became merely another factor which had to be considered. If we wanted to amend the fourth year options, time was not only spent upon the effect the changes would have on other subjects, or the increase or decrease in choice given to pupils, or the effect upon the sixth form curriculum, but realistic accounting of the cost of such changes of staff or resources was demanded before decisions were taken.

The development in the system reflected this philosophical evolution. Initially, I wanted to devise a scheme which utilised as far as possible the present system, satisfied the staff's concern about the use of the money, and involved the governors in the financial decision-making of the school. We were very fortunate in that the accounts department were already accustomed to a more sophisticated method of accounting of the capitation and over the previous 12 years had been concerned with administering considerable capital sums spent on equipping and furnishing new suites of rooms as the school had been extended.

During that time major building projects had been completed which changed the school from a complex consisting of a relatively small permanent building and 25 mobile classrooms to a modern complex of permanent building suites able to accommodate 1500 main school pupils and 150 6th form students. That experience, and the ability to order goods direct, check goods and delivery slips, attach correctly coded payment slips to invoices and forward them with confidence to Shire Hall, proved invaluable. The extra load placed upon the administrative accounts staff was, therefore, minimal. The departmental accounts filing system developed over the last twelve years helped them to check fairly easily the monthly print-outs of expenditure.

Two major problems have been: the late arrivals of these monthly sheets and the inability, in the early stages, of Shire Hall to give a date before which all invoices should be included in the printout. Our accounts staff would find that some invoices sent in on the 20th of the month were excluded, while invoices sent in on the 24th were included. To a large extent this has now been rectified. One benefit which we certainly reaped was the reduction in the number of second invoices demanding payment being sent by suppliers. Because payment slips were sent direct to Shire Hall, payment was made more quickly, thus releasing my staff from the drudgery of having to check second demands.

Management structure within the school

At the academic staff level there already existed a series of management bodies, and each department held its own subject departmental meetings. The heads of department came together each fortnight under my leadership to discuss wider curriculum matters in a *Board of Studies*. The heads of year met their group tutors regularly and for pastoral policy matters met me in the *Pastoral Board* each week. The *Executive*, consisting of my three deputies and myself and staff responsible for specific matters, such as the staff tutor and examinations officer, met to discuss the overall planning and organisation of the school.

The first question was to decide whether to use this existing system or to create a new system especially for financial matters. In the event we chose the former, but added a *Monitoring committee* for finance based upon union representation. The success of adding finance to the existing committees' agenda was so great that the monitoring exercise by the unions' representatives gradually became defunct. Although its demise was hastened by the more recent industrial action, the usefulness of the body had already been questioned and no-one has asked for its resurrection.

The fear that the new scheme would give enormous powers to the head has now largely subsided and been replaced by a more positive and constructive approach by heads of department and heads of year. A number of factors have combined to revolutionise these meetings. First, prior to the scheme being introduced, discussions were predominantly consultative. Staff felt that whatever consensus was achieved, implementation depended upon the area office or Shire Hall staff giving permission. They saw the head as the link or obstacle to that implementation. They believed, quite wrongly, that ideas I supported were pressed upon the LEA, while ideas I opposed were not so encouragingly supported, ensuring that a negative result came from Shire Hall.

Second, staff in this middle-management area now feel that the discussions are comprehensive in their meetings. Papers are produced, costings made, rival claims discussed and at the conclusion a decision is reached and ultimately introduced. Staff are prepared to be more factual and much more realistic because they have to live with their colleagues who know whether they opposed or supported the scheme. Thus in preparing the budget for 1986/87, the year GCSE was introduced, real arguments ensued as to whether greater capitation or more ancillary support staff was required. Science staff, who wanted more technician time, found that history, geography and modern language staff also wanted clerical support. Other departments required money to be included for supply staff while they carried out oral tests, and others demanded more equipment and more books. It was fascinating to notice the demand for accurate costings of each request, the very strong counter arguments by one department against another and the real anger provoked by one head of department who tried to kill the discussion by vague, antiquated and irrelevant generalisation.

Problem areas

These realistic, meaningful and decision-making meetings of heads of department and heads of year have had adverse effects upon two groups. There is no doubt that heads of department and heads of year feel that they are participating much more effectively in the overall planning and organisation of the school. But as their feeling of participation has increased, the staff below head of department level have felt omitted and excluded from participation. I think that this has been caused first by staff feeling that they must have direct involvement in the decision-making exercise — unless they are members of a group where the head is present they do not feel consulted. Second, some heads of department have been so concerned with the problem of GCSE that their meetings have concentrated upon methods of testing, new schemes of work, modified teaching techniques, and they have not discussed with members of their department the topics and financial implications on the Board of Studies agenda. Both problems have to be solved: staff have to learn that views may have to be expressed by their head of department, and that they must trust the head of department to do so. In the same way I must trust the heads of department to communicate accurately both ways – to members of the department, and to me. Time and practice, I am sure, can solve this matter.

The second group of staff whose position could be undermined by the effect of the LFM consultation procedures is the Executive who risk being in a no-man's-land within the decision-making process. In the former 'top-down system', a proposal emanating from the Executive would be 'sold' to the middle-tier management, putting the Executive in a key position. Now that so many decisions are made at the Board of Studies and Pastoral Board meetings, there is a danger that the Executive could become nothing more than a routine administrative group, solving or evading the short-term crisis: staff cover, an individual teacher's problems, poor decorative state of certain buildings and so on. All these are matters which have to be dealt with, of course, but if a deputy's role is reduced to these factors, frustration and dissatisfaction could set in.

We are trying to solve this unforeseen problem in a number of ways which may restore the diminished self-image of the Executive team. We need to ensure that longer-term planning features on the agenda of our regular meetings and that more informal discussions take place. In addition, it is important to give each Deputy an 'exciting' new project to lead, such as the introduction of TVEI, primary school liaison, or work experience for 4th years.

The involvement of governors

I have outlined the effect of the scheme upon the accounts department and upon the middle management level of the academic staff. The third element which needed to be involved effectively was the Governing Body. Traditionally the governors had met once a term to receive the head's report and to receive a governors' report on the state of the buildings. This system was totally unsuitable for governor involvement in Local Financial Management, in which the LEA had delegated to the head and to the governors the task of controlling the school's finances. Consequently, the governors decided to create a Finance Sub-Committee consisting of the Chairman and Vice-Chairman and four members, of which one must be a staff governor. The constitution of the body is as follows:

GOVERNOR'S FINANCE SUB-COMMITTEE CONSTITUTION

1   *Election of members to committees*
   a Suggested committee membership should be produced by Chairman and Vice-Chairman prior to the January meeting of each year: to elect such Committees for the October meeting would not be possible as Chairman and Vice-Chairman are not elected until the October meeting.
   b Full Governors' meeting to ratify or refute committee membership.
2 TERMS OF OFFICE
   a Committee membership should be for one year in duration.
   b Members available for committees: three members and at least one staff governor on the Finance Sub-Committee.
   c No Governor should be re-elected for the same Sub-Committee for more than three years.
   d The Chairman and Vice-Chairman of the Governors shall be *ex-officio* members of the Sub-Committees.
   e That the Vice-Chairman shall be Chairman of the Finance Sub-Committee.
3 TERMS OF REFERENCE for Finance Sub-Committee shall be as follows:
   a That the Sub-Committee should have executive powers.

b That the Sub-Committee should report their actions and/or recommendations to the full Governors' meeting each term.
c To analyse the monthly expenditure and running total of the LFM print-out and to take corrective action if the urgency of the situation demands it.
d To make or anticipate the making of decisions concerning virement of funds in accordance with the authority vested in the Sub-Committee.
e To consider and review the school fund accounts.
f The headmaster to provide papers on all matters prior to the meetings.
g There shall be monthly meetings of the Sub-Committee to meet on the last Friday of each month or any suitable day.

The governors have met regularly on a monthly basis. Two distinct types of meeting have evolved. During the period February to June the meetings are primarily concerned with creating and modifying the budget. The budget is created by March but modified as the previous year's balances are added, and financial repurcussions of staff movement are calculated. The second type of financial meeting is between June and January, when the governors are more concerned with monitoring the progress of the spending in relation to the anticipated budget demands. To strengthen still further the view that the scheme has gone beyond financial matters, the governors have now set up three further committees: one concerned with staffing matters, the second concerned with pupils' discipline and welfare and the third concerned with the buildings and grounds. Each meet either regularly or as required, eg to appoint staff. Specialist knowledge has been developed; governors are much more aware of the life of the school, and are giving significantly more time to school matters. I have been fortunate that the quality of governor has been such that they have relished the new responsibilities. Fine distinctions have to be made, however, between overall planning and interference in the day to day administration of the school. The termly full Governors' Meeting now receives chairman's reports from each of the sub-committees on finance, staff, pupils and buildings; this allows the head's report to be concerned with curriculum development, long-term plans or major specific problems.

Creating the budget

It is significant that during the years of the pilot scheme staff attitude to the budget has changed – from the perception that it controlled the life and thinking of the school to the view that the budget is used to implement curriculum decisions. In the autumn term the Board of Studies leads a series of discussions over the curriculum needs for the next academic year. In 1986 we decided to study three specific areas. First, having introduced GCSE in the fourth year we began to understand two major requirements following on from that change. It became obvious that our schemes of work in the first three years needed to be modified. Modern language graded tests were introduced in German as well as French, the science subjects' material was modified. Furthermore, real concern was expressed about the need to increase ancillary support staff across the whole curriculum. Suggested changes were costed and given a priority status when budgetary decisions were to be made.

The second issue was to study the fourth and fifth year curriculum, to attempt to increase the efficiency of the use of staff without decreasing pupil choice. As a result of these discussions we introduced a curriculum which ensured that all pupils in the fourth and fifth would study English, mathematics, a foreign language, two sciences, a humanities and two further subjects, either to bring in a second foreign language or a third science or subjects from the craft or aesthetic band, plus PE, RE, and a social and personal development period. This change was given top priority when the budget was created. The staffing requirements were calculated for the whole of the 11–18 age range; using the staff we had and the changes we anticipated, the final cost of the staff to introduce that curriculum was recorded.

The second priority of ancillary support staff was then calculated and it was decided to give support hours to humanities and languages departments. In previous years extra technician hours had been allocated to the craft department and to the reprographics section. It is vital to note that where extra staff are allocated at academic or ancillary level, an on-going cost has to be assumed. We were committing ourselves to future costs by accepting these staffing improvements. The curriculum demands also showed a need for 2.5 academic staff more than the LEA were offering to us. Perhaps the greatest success in the scheme is that since 1982 we have used from .6 to 2.5 academic staff above the county establishment for the school. We have also reached the goal of curriculum-led staffing. The total staffing cost is completed in March by calculating total ancillary, caretaking, cleaning and foreign language assistant staff and assessing the supply needs.

Document A shows the build-up of our present budget. The three columns show changes made between March and June. The original was based upon a total budget of £1,337,270 given by the LEA. Three changes have been made. The first two reflect increases in the budget by the allocation of £4530 GCSE money and £17185 carried forward from the 1986/87 budget. The third change is the result of staff movement during the summer term. Each time a member of staff moves

DOCUMENT A

School Expenditure and Income Financial Year 1987/88 – Budget

	ESTIMATE	B	C	D	E
	£				
EMPLOYEES					
0110 Full Time/School P–T	985,000	990,000	995,000		
0112 Supply (Not Mat/Vacs)	12,000	12,000	12,000		
0114 Supply – For Maternity	—	—	—	—	—
0118 Supply – For Vacancies		—	—	—	—
0120 Admin/Prof/Clerical	40,000	39,000+2475	41,475		
0124 Lab/Tech/Welfare/Gen	20,000	19,000	19,000		
0141 Caretakers–Educ & SS	20,000	21,000	21,000		
0142 Cleaners–Educ Only	29,000	29,000	29,000		
0179 Other incl FLAs	2,900	2,900	2,900		
	1,108,900	1,112,900+2475	1,120,375		
PREMISES					
1320 Oil	18,000	18,000	18,000		
1330 Electricity	12,000	12,000	12,000		
1340 Gas-Mains	6,000	6,000	6,000		
1350 Water Rates		—		—	
1351 Water Charges	4,000	4,000	4,000		
1360 Cleaning Materials	3,000	3,000	3,000		

DOCUMENT A *(continued)*

School Expenditure and Income Financial Year 1987/88 – Budget

	ESTIMATE	B	C	D	E
PREMISES	£				
1370 Window Cleaning	750	750	750		
1391 Refuse Collection	750	750	750		
1420 Fnture Pchse/£5550	—	—	—		
1540 General Rates	80,000	75,550	75,550		
1541 Sewerage Rates	4,000	4,000	4,000		
	128,500	124,050	124,050		
SUPPLIES & SERVICES					
2110 General-under £6000	—	—	—		
2600 Capitation Allowances	92,640	108,560	108,560		
2780 Protective Clothing	200	200	200		
2800 Laundry	130	200	200		
Buildings	4,000	4,000	4,000		
Contingency		10,000	5,000		
	97,170	122,960	117,960		

TRANSPORT & MOVBLE PL			
3110 Car Allowances	1,000	1,000	1,000
	1,000	1,000	1,000
ESTABLISHMENT EXPENSES			
4031 Internal Printing	—	—	—
4040 Advertising for Staff	1,500	1,500	1,500
4110 Staff Trav & Subsist	200	200	200
	1,700	1,700	1,700
Income	−6,100	−6,100	−6,100
	−6,100	−6,100	−6,100
TOTAL EXPENDITURE	£1,337,270	£1,358,985	£1,358,985
BUDGET	£1,337,270	£1,341,800	
BALANCE 1986/87		17,185.39	
TOTAL REVENUE:		£1,358,985.39	

the cost to the staffing budget also changes. This can involve an increase or a decrease in that budget heading. A further complexity arose this year with the anticipated introduction in October of the second phase of the salary increase. I decided that a small sum should be added to the staff budget as a contingency against any shortfall in financial allocation by the LEA for that increase. If the LEA added a percentage increase to my salary bill and that percentage was less than the actual cost of the salary increase to my staff, the small additional income would be useful. If the allocated sum was accurate I would then be in a position to re-allocate that sum later in the year. It is noticeable that 83.5% of the total budget is taken up in staffing costs.

The budget for the second major heading of premises is created by an assessment of costing based upon historical data, and known procedures to save money. This year we are attempting to reduce lighting costs by repeating an in-school advertising campaign to switch off lights and by installing key switches in corridors to stop corridor lights being switched on when they are not required. We are also inviting independent tenders for the cleaning of windows and have already reduced the cost of refuse collection by using private contractors rather than the service provided by the district council.

The amounts allocated to transport and establishment expenses and the anticipated revenue from lettings and joint use of our premises produce a relatively small figure. The balance is then allocated to the supplies and services section, of which the major heading is capitation. The heads of department, pastoral heads, head of administration and staff such as examinations officer provide me with a detailed request for sums to administer their department during the coming year.

Individual discussions take place and each department and each item within the department's request is given a priority. Thus, if one department wishes to introduce a new third year textbook then the cost of that introduction must either be accepted in full or not at all. To give a percentage of that sum would inhibit the introduction of the book. However, if the English department wishes to purchase carpets for eight rooms, a decision may be reached where four may be carpeted in 1987/88 and four in 1988/89. To create confidence, total openness is essential. The department budget (as illustrated) is printed and distributed to all members of staff. During this period of February to June the Governors' Finance Committee vets the recommendations and make the final budget. It is not until they have formally accepted the figures and their effect upon the life of the school that the budget is passed to the LEA.

During the year monthly printouts are received from Shire Hall. The summary sheets are checked by me. It is not that I need accountancy skills, but I do need to be aware of trends. If a particular heading shows a different picture to the one expected I make a detailed check. On the June, 1987 summary printout (Document B) there is a balance in 0110 Staffing of £9,136.90. This was unexpected and my investigations revealed that one member of staff had been wrongly coded and, therefore, her salary had not been debited to St Peter's.

The summary sheet shows Total Budget, Anticipated Budget to Date, Actual Cost to Date and the difference between Anticipated Budget and Actual Cost. At the moment the target figures in column 2 do not accurately reflect the spending pattern in individual schools. There is no point in dividing Capitation into twelve equal parts and assuming the spending pattern is even over the whole year. A great proportion is spent between April and September. In the same way heating and lighting costs are much less in the summer than in the winter. Even staff costings are not equally spread, for the cost is different after September when increments are paid and when the staff establishment may be changed. Trend watching has to be aware of these anomalies. Certainly any future computer programme must reflect more accurately the spending pattern.

A major problem is the difficulty of reconciling supply staff payments as numbers, not names, appear on the detailed printout. Schemes are being introduced to marry payment numbers with staff names so that each school can verify that they are paying for supply staff actually used in their particular establishment. The detailed printout of payments for goods, etc, is checked by the accounts department. This takes approximately three hours each month and is easily compensated for by the work saved in not having to process repeat payment demands because of the more speedy payment of accounts by Shire Hall. A further problem has arisen where heads of department use inaccurate costings in their requisitions. One result has been that capitation purchases have been stopped in December because of overspending by some departments when invoices show major differences between requisition and actual payments. The departments who have underspent have lost their unspent allocation because of the overspending of others. This year, therefore, a graduated spending pattern has been designed for all departments. 75% of their capitation may be spent by September 1st, a further 20% may be spent by December 1st and the remainder by the end of the financial year. Thus departments who have used inaccurate costings do not have to be subsidised by the other departments.

DOCUMENT B

Cambridgeshire LFM Scheme – Schools
Expenditure and Income for the period ended June 1987

318 07/07/87
8007 Huntgdn St Peter's

	Revised Total Budget for year £	Expected to date £	Actual to date £	Variation to date £
Employees				
0110 Full Time Teachers	1,069,672	270,626	261,489.10	9,136,90–
0112 Casual Supply Tchrs	12,776	3,653	920.08	2,732.92–
0113 Repl Tchers on Traing			52.30	52.30
0114 GCSE Inset Funds	4,816	963	2,345.03	1,382.03
0120 Support Staff	60,475	15,385	11,280.36	4,104.64–
0141 Caretakers	20,806	5,212	5,940.70	728.70
0142 Cleaners	29,000	7,250	7,509.48	259.48
0179 For Lang Assts etc	2,900	787	852.48	65.48
	1,200,445	303,876	290,389.53	13,486.47–
Premises				
1118 Alterations-LFM Schs	4,000		.00	.00
1320 Oil	13,772	4,885	5,441.22	556.22

1330	Electricity	12,000	2,651	2,260.52	390.48–
1340	Gas-Mains	6,000	1,685	96.71	1,588.29–
1351	Water Charges	4,000	1,344	3,367.94	2,023.94
1360	Cleaning Materials	3,289	802	252.59	549.41–
1370	Window Cleaning	770	188	.00	188.00–
1391	Refuse Collection	774	189	185.50	3.50–
1540	General Rates	75,550	22,665	35,139.50	12,474.50
1541	Sewerage Rates	4,000	1,343	.00	1,343.00–
		124,155	35,752	46,743.98	10,991.98

Supplies & Services

2600	Capitation Allownces	98,622	19,057	42,080.44	23,023.44
		98,622	19,057	42,080.44	23,023.44

Transport & Mvble Pl

3110	Car Allowances	1,021	255	191.12	63.88–
		1,021	255	191.12	63.88–

DOCUMENT B *(continued)*

Cambridgeshire LFM Scheme – Schools
Expenditure and Income for the period ended June 1987

318 07/07/87
8007 Huntgdn St Peter's

	Revised Total Budget for year £	Expected to date £	Actual to date £	Variation to date £
Establshmnt Expenses				
4040 Advertising for Staf	1,534	375	235.32	139.68 –
4110 Staff Trav & Subsist	200	49	16.55	32.45 –
	1,734	424	251.87	172.13 –
Miscellaneous Exps				
Total Expenditure	1,425,977	359,364	379,656.94	20,292.94

Income				
8420 Casual Lettings			39.85–	39.85–
8421 Ctkrs/Clnrs Etc Fees			60.60–	60.60–
8422 Heat & Light Charge			39.85–	39.85–
			140.30–	140.30–
Recharges				
9211 Premises Recharged	6,100–		.00	.00
	6,100–		.00	.00
Net Expenditure	1,419,877	359,364	379,516.64	20,152.64

Positive outcomes

The results of the scheme have been significant. Easily quantifiable are those areas where we have provided more than would have been provided by the LEA in pre-LFM days. The most important has been the increase and flexibility in staffing. Since 1982 we have had from 0.6 to 2.5 academic staff above establishment. A further improvement has been the fiexible attitude towards appointment and resignation of staff. One member of the Technology Department resigned on October 30th, 1986. It was impossible to appoint before Easter. However, the school from which our new member of staff was coming asked that he stayed with them until June 1st, 1987 in order to maintain the 'A' level studies. As we had coped for one term but wanted him to be present for the new timetable, which in our school begins in July, we agreed. In a different context a very loyal long-serving member of staff asked to be released at the end of the summer term, although the May 31st deadline had passed. Again because of this new, flexible approach, I agreed and successfully appointed a probationer to start in September.

Twenty more technician hours and 40 more clerical ancillary hours are being used each week. Capitation allocation is considerably higher than the figures produced by the LEA. This year £108 000 will be spent on capitation for a school population of just under 1300. A 16-station computer laboratory, a technology room and a design centre have all been developed. Computers have been installed in the administrative wing and carpets have been laid in all the modern language rooms and some of the English rooms. A 43-seater coach was purchased to help in extra-curricular activities; we are now gaining the benefit of the purchase as it has reduced the cost of theatre visits, games fixtures and fieldwork.

Of even greater importance, but much less quantifiable, has been the change in staff approach. Decision-making is more positive. Staff realise that they can participate actively and directly in the allocation of money and, therefore, in the total management of the school. Innovations suggested by staff must be costed and this results in a greater realism in suggested changes. This feeling of being part of the controlling management of the school has meant a willingness on the part of staff to be involved in self-help projects. The design centre was developed by the technology department in association with the county's maintenance engineers. The refurbishing of a science laboratory has resulted from a team effort: physics staff planning, technology staff building the benches, maintenance engineers providing expertise and the school providing money for gas and electricity installation.

While the work load on administrative staff has risen only marginally, the increased consultative time demanded of me has been significant. But these discussions have brought enormous benefits and have resulted in implemented schemes being more accurate and more worthwhile. There has been an increase in my administrative work load, in the calculation of budget changes, and in the monthly monitoring procedure. I would suggest, however, that this is a small price to pay for the increased efficiency and improved resources gained by the school.

Relationships outside the school

Relations between heads and officers of the county have undergone considerable change. For twelve years the Chief Education Officer has consulted with heads through the Standing Committee of the Cambridgeshire Association of Secondary Heads. While I was chairman of that Committee, I felt it was a consultative but not a participative exercise. Although ideas for bodies consisting of officers, heads and inspectors were expressed, they never materialised. Local Financial Management has created this unifying force. The seven pilot schools have been members of a committee consisting of a deputy education officer, finance officers, heads, elected members and chairmen of governors. With the extension of the scheme to all secondary schools, cluster groupings have been set up consisting of the education and finance officers, heads, chairmen of governors and one elected member. I hope that inspectors will be included in the future. The result has been a greater understanding of each other's problems. School and Shire Hall officers have come together with a greater understanding of each others' problems and requests. With a few exceptions, no longer do we see polarised situations created; no longer do we perceive a reluctance to produce full information; and perhaps most significantly, we do not have a sense of distrust between heads and officers of Shire Hall.

Just as groups within the school altered their roles, so the area office has been forced to modify its role. In the administrative field it no longer checks payment slips, or participates in the checking and forwarding of lettings bills. Those schools which have extended LFM to school meals or have received property bursars have reduced their administrative involvement with the local 'office'. More importantly, at the management level, the area officer no longer plays an effective role in the creation of the staff budget by allocating to each school a staff establishment.

Future changes?

I have tried to reflect the great changes in the management of St Peter's School which have followed the introduction of LFM but good schemes create pressures for further change as well as bringing alterations in their wake. LFM has increased an awareness of the total management of the school and a team approach to the daily routine of school administration. It has also shown the real value of making decisions and controlling factors at the local level. It appears, therefore, anomalous to exclude minor maintenance of buildings, the upkeep of grounds and school meals from the scheme. The next steps should be to break down the isolationism of the property department and to devolve to the heads, in consultation with property bursars, at least two of these three elements of school administration.

Distribution of budget

Another result of LFM has been to highlight the real differences between unit costs of differing establishments. In 1985/86 the pupil unit cost in Cambridgeshire varied from just over £900 to more than £1400. This inequity is unjust. Long accepted prejudices that small schools must be subsidised by large schools, or that special factors, such as social need, split sites, old buildings, country or urban problems, have to be evaluated in order to create individual budgets, should be brought under the questioning scrutiny of a formal inquiry. It is necessary to study the formal curriculum of schools, especially at 4th and 5th year levels, to see whether staff are being used economically and effectively. Heads who have, in the past, been accorded privileged status by being given high pupil unit costs, should participate in the reassessment of the total situation and not merely defend the status quo. One of the great benefits of LFM has been the effect it has had on unexpected areas. This costing inequality is one of those areas. I favour very strongly the idea of a small specific allocation for rates and specific needs, such as GCSE, INSET, TVEI and Section11: the remainder to be allocated either on an age-weighted pupil unit or on a form of entry basis weighted by years. The weighting and balance between the first three years, years four and five, and the sixth and seventh years, can be accurately calculated to reflect the curriculum needs of these three areas. To create a scheme such as LFM and then to miss the opportunity of making fair and just amendments to the distribution of the budget to schools would be a real weakness and a sad omission.

Questions for discussion

1   *If LFM were being introduced to your school, would you adopt George Thomas's approach of using the existing management structure rather than creating a new and separate system for financial matters? Justify your choice.*

2   *In terms of staff relations, George Thomas highlights two problem areas. If you were responsible for setting up LFM in your school, how would you avoid these problems?*

3   *If you compare the governors' finance sub-committee constitution with the Financial Management Committee pattern given in Part One (page 31), you will see that the significant difference is in the number of teaching staff directly involved in negotiations with the governors. Which approach do you agree with? Do you think that the difference is significant?*

4   *The distribution of 'capitation' to departments is done by a system of bids and priority decisions. An alternative method is to devise an in-school formula for distribution, based on the number of pupils taking the subject. Members of the group may have experienced both systems; discuss their relative strengths and weaknesses. Is it inconsistent for a head who believes in formula distribution from LEA to school not to adopt the same approach to distribution within school?*

5   *George Thomas gives a number of examples of how he has improved on staffing by making savings in staffing at certain times in the year. How acceptable do you think colleagues in the schools you know would find this approach? If they were critical of it how might you go about persuading them to change their minds?*

6   *One of the criticisms of LFM is that the increased workload on heads would be unacceptable to them. What aspects of George Thomas's article would you use to refute that criticism?*

7   *It is sometimes suggested that the main administrative saving achieved by the adoption of LFM will be in jobs at area office which appears to have a diminished role in an LEA with financial autonomy in its schools. In the LEA with which you are familiar, what functions of the area office, if any, would you wish to see retained?*

8   *Simulate a discussion at a secondary school which finds that it has overspent by £12 000 and will have to cut back to that amount*

in the following year. Make sure that the views of head, teacher governor, parent governor, non-teaching staff representative are heard.

Chapter 5 Implementing LFM across a whole Local Education Authority

David Hill

With the benefit of having worked on both 'sides' of LFM, as Head and as an LEA Officer, David Hill suggests practical steps that should be considered by LEAs as they move, voluntarily or under central government direction, towards a scheme of delegated financial responsibility. After a brief reminder of the national perspective, he looks at the implications for an LEA and for governors, and draws attention to a number of organisational problems which need to be anticipated. David Hill goes on to consider the difficult area of community education within LFM and recommends a solution which not all will find easy to accept. Although his article does not seek to disguise the actual and potential problems, his personal conclusion is an optimistic and encouraging one.

The national perspective

In July 1987, the Secretary of State published a consultation paper for local education authorities developing the Government's proposals to introduce legislation later in the year. These proposals lead to the introduction of a scheme to

- ensure that the parents and the community know on what basis the available resources are distributed in their area and how much is being spent on each school;
- give the governors of all county and voluntary secondary schools, and of larger primary schools, freedom to take expenditure decisions which match their own priorities, and the guarantee that their own school will benefit if they achieve efficiency savings.

The Government's plans place LEAs under a new duty to devise schemes of financial delegation, with their proposals being submitted to the Secretary of State by September 1989.

Prior to 1987 a number of local education authorities had introduced some degree of local autonomy into their schools. All schools were familiar with control over their capitation for books, equipment and various other small items, but this would be less than 5% of the total cost of running a school. Heads and governors were also experienced in appointing teachers and support staff within certain boundaries of a salary structure but they were seldom aware of the actual cost of the person appointed. All financial matters were usually dealt with centrally by officers and accountants at a county or town hall.

LEAs approached moves to delegate wider financial responsibilities to schools in a variety of ways. The most radical were those in which responsibility for more than 75% of the total budget was given to heads and governors. Some authorities were unwilling to be so radical and only increased slightly the responsibility delegated. These latter schemes excluded teacher salaries – which, in the view of the more radical authorities, would not lead to a significant change in the role of heads and governors. Other authorities would not delegate any items above capitation, wishing to maintain strict central control for the officers and councillors. It is also apparent that in some authorities, the treasury is extremely reluctant for delegation to take place. Some accountants (and some education officers) appear to be extremely concerned about their headteachers' capabilities to manage a budget – this despite the fact that the head is often on a higher salary than the accountant or officer concerned and, in the case of a secondary head, is directly responsible for a building and a large number of employees.

It should not be forgotten that most aspiring heads have almost certainly attended a number of management courses. They most certainly are capable of such activities as
- understanding what is provided and how much is spent;
- initiating work to reconsider resource allocation;
- assessing alternatives and their cost;
- consulting with those staff affected and those officers properly involved;
- deciding whether to change, and what, when and how;
- evaluating the effectiveness of the change.

A problem of the state education scene in recent years has been the stifling of headteachers by local education authorities. Some LEAs appoint people to these senior posts and then, with ever-increasing bureaucracy, ensure that they have little freedom in which to manage.

Of course, increased responsibility will create more of a risk situation both for the LEA and head, but many heads strongly welcome this.

The LEA perspective

Before embarking on a new scheme, LEAs will be wise to take notice of a statement in the Secretary of State's consultation paper:

The Government believes that it will be essential in the development of wider financial delegation to schools that full account is taken of the experience and expertise already developed by local government needs and circumstances.

Authorities with experience of devolution have been developing their schemes at their own pace over a number of years. Those without such experience may not be allowed by the Government to progress as slowly. The scheme in Cambridgeshire, though highly successful, has had many teething problems and prior knowledge of such problems can help other authorities to move at a quicker pace. At the outset, in 1982, Cambridgeshire appointed an external assessor and authorities are advised to use this type of consultancy service for a few days each year.

It does seem that it is preferable to start with a pilot scheme including many budget areas, rather than with all schools gradually building up the number of delegated budget areas each year. The latter approach may well leave teacher salaries until last, as this area could give the greatest problems, but the scheme would remain without real management at the school level until this happened.

It needs to be emphasised over and over again that the scheme should have positive benefits for the pupil in the classroom. Experience suggests that this will happen but that it takes at least two years before the benefits become noticeable. This will lead governors and headteachers, who may express many initial reservations, to become more enthusiastic as the scheme progresses.

As the budget is 'opened up' many issues will be raised. Heads have noticed that many problems are resolved in the first year, but new ones do appear and are often of a more complex nature than hitherto.

The scheme will increase the trust between governors, heads, officers and councillors as all become more aware of each other's problems. Many councillors are also school governors and they will find it most illuminating to see a detailed analysis of their school's budgets. Heads will learn that the county budget is cash limited and that officers and councillors have to plan years in advance to make major changes to the budget. Heads and governors quickly realise that, given the school's total budget for the year, it is pointless requesting additional funds during the year. Schools, like the LEA, have to manage within the allocated cash limit.

Headteachers do not have to become biased towards accountancy or administration. The scheme is about local management and it aims to increase the management aspect of the head's role. As with any senior manager, she or he will need accountants and administrative staff to advise and do the paperwork, but the head, with governors and senior staff, is involved primarily with decision-taking.

Using an 'implementation team'

In 1986, Cambridgeshire decided to allocate a small amount of the education budget to setting up an implementation team for two years. A pilot school headteacher was appointed to be the team leader, with his deputy being a qualified accountant. The leader was responsible for training and advising heads and governors, for advising officers, and for the general development of the scheme. He gave at least one presentation at every school entering the scheme and attended all governor's meetings, with a follow-up, if requested, at staff, parent, or community meetings. He also attended regular half-termly meetings with a committee of the teachers' consultative council, representing the teacher unions, and with a committee representing the heads. The team leader arranged for termly meetings of heads and chairmen of governors in clusters of approximately nine schools each. These meetings were each chaired by a member of the County Council Working Group on LFM. Initially, the meetings were used by schools to register small individual complaints, but they soon settled down to discussing major issues, with schools making many positive contributions.

The team leader raised LFM issues at county officers' management team meetings, attended by senior officers and inspectors. An LFM officers' group, consisting of the team leader and deputy team leader, Deputy Chief Education Officer, Assistant Director of Finance and Administration, an education finance officer, a senior area education officer, a secondary and a primary inspector and an auditor, met fortnightly. From this meeting, major issues were taken to the management team and to the councillors' LFM working group.

Three other team members were appointed – each to take responsibility for 19 schools. These were three young accountant technicians, chosen on both their administrative ability and their personality. They were to check the monthly printouts sent to each school and respond to individual questions. The three spent time in each school familiaris-ing themselves with the financial arrangements, and quickly became more closely involved with each of the schools, being seen as an additional resource. What was not anticipated was that many schools expected them to attend their finance meetings. As these meetings were usually in the evenings, the young accountants were having to do much evening work – unusual for an officer on their salary scale. They were also expected to discuss issues with heads and with finance committees, and they found this task daunting at first. Fortunately, the personality and professionalism of these young officers enabled them to adapt quickly to these new experiences.

The deputy team leader was responsible for the work of the team members and for the training of secondary school finance officers. A series of training meetings was held, as there was considerable variety in the quality of administrative staff in the schools. These meetings proved to be the first county-wide training sessions for school administration that had been organised. Previous policy appeared to be that the training of school administrative staff had always been left to the heads of schools. Many schools heeded the advice of the LFM team to restructure their school office. A separate finance officer, as distinct from a secretary, was required. Schools advertising these posts on relatively low salaries found no shortage of applicants, from people who had been trained as bank clerks or those seeking part-time employment after early retirement.

The deputy team leader worked with the central computer division to help to produce a suitable programme for school office computers. The County Council did not provide schools with computers, but many had purchased one or two for their office and needed advice and training for their staff. The deputy leader also assisted with pro-ducing statistical information required for research into budget issues and the formula approach to LFM. Cambridgeshire and IBM have recently combined in an attempt to have a full financial software package available (to all LEAs) early in 1988.

Primary schools usually did not have an administrator who dealt with financial issues. In most primary schools, and in all smaller ones, the headteacher dealt with these issues personally. It was usually the headteacher who actually had to administer orders, invoices and related matters. The LFM team advises that better value for money would be obtained if headteachers could be released from these clerical tasks, with part-time clerical assistants being appointed.

All schools reported on the valuable assistance provided by the

LFM implementation team. They particularly appreciated the team member role. Heads stated that it was refreshing to be able to deal directly with one officer only on all financial matters, and to have a central officer who spent much time at the school, enabling them to understand fully their individual problems. They liked the speed of response from the team member who was often able to reply within one day to queries raised. They trusted the team member, who was, in turn, trusted by central finance officers. Centrally, the team members knew the personnel and the method of working, which enabled them to research and answer problems raised by the school without undue delay.

The development of this role is to be encouraged. Such posts need to remain after the implementation process has finished, and can be achieved by the reduction of other central finance posts. Authorities, though, will find it very difficult to bring about a reduction in central administrative posts. Central personnel are often unwilling to concede that resources should be transferred from the centre to individual establishments. They may not easily accept the need to change.

The role of governors

The scheme does give an improved role to governors. In pilot schools in Cambridgeshire, governors have welcomed their increased responsibilities and the opportunity to become really involved in the management of the school, in partnership with the head and staff.

In most cases the governing body has formed a sub-committee to deal with financial matters, obviating the need for all to take a detailed interest. This has often been the impetus for governors to form a number of sub-committees, dealing with such areas as curriculum, buildings, staffing and welfare. The agenda for the main governors' meeting can then mainly comprise discussion of reports from the sub-committee chairmen. Individual governors have enjoyed the experience of being able to specialise in one area only of the school, especially if they have previously been somewhat overwhelmed by the amount of expertise required, especially in a secondary school. Sub-committees consist of governors and ex-officio staff, and it is not necessary for the head to be involved with all the committees. Deputy heads welcome the experience of being the senior member of staff present.

It is not necessary for the governors on the finance sub-committee to be financial experts. Their main role is to discuss the management decisions recommended by the staff and then to ensure that the costs involved have been carefully planned. Governors from industry and commerce fully understand this procedure and find it refreshing to take part in such discussions.

The local community soon learns that being a governor of a school can be worthwhile and this leads to an improvement in the quality of those prepared to stand for election. Parent governors in particular are very keen to serve on the finance committee. Realisation that a governing body has ultimate responsibility is very stimulating and does release energy and goodwill.

Problems

An initial problem will be to provide schools with the detailed information that is required. Information technology is still in a development stage in most LEAs. Some schools have purchased personal computers for their offices and in some authorities these are linked to a central mainframe. An alternative system, as used in Cambridgeshire, is to develop software to be used in school offices, with back-up from a monthly printout giving budget headings, with annual budget, profile budget, amount spent to date and the variation from the profile. These printouts are seen by the head, governors and staff. A second detailed printout gives all items of expenditure and income in the previous month, to be checked by the finance secretary. Other printouts give details of staff salaries, both teaching and non-teaching. Work is taking place in Cambridgeshire to improve the format further.

At first, the workload for those involved at the school may be greater than originally envisaged but this is probably due to the learning process. There needs to be an initial training programme. The LEA should ensure that each governing body has an opportunity to discuss their new responsibilities under Local Financial Management. Meetings need to be arranged in each school with an officer (ideally the implementation team leader) giving information and allowing opportunity for discussion, questions and answers. It would be sensible if such a meeting was also open to staff and parents. Literature, including guidelines, needs to be available. The officer leading the meeting needs to be enthusiastic and positive but should not ignore the problem areas.

Headteachers need less training for the introduction of the scheme than is generally thought by those without real knowledge of how it works. LFM is about management rather than finance, and headteachers should already have experience of management training. They may, however, wish to receive training in understanding the financial processes involved. The scheme emphasises consultation and open information, and most modern headteachers will be familiar with this attitude to decision making, although very autocratic heads (if there are any!) may find it difficult to adjust.

Administrative staff in schools will have the greatest training needs. They will have to understand the procedures required and it is in this area that the LFM team members can play a vital role. Without doubt, all school offices will be computerised within the next decade. This will be of concern to some school secretaries who fear that they have a computer phobia and will not be able to cope. Such secretaries need careful and sympathetic training. The changing roles in the school office can lead to tension and the transition does require good management, by both the LEA and by the school.

Local Financial Management will expose the underfunding of certain areas of the budget. Education authority budgets are often balanced by using unexpected large underspendings to underwrite a number of small overspendings, and some of these overspendings may have been allowed to continue for a number of years. Schools will soon spot these areas of overspendings in their base budget and will demand that the budget is increased. At the same time, schools would be incensed should the authority try to reclaim any of the fortuitous underspendings to finance the overspendings. With this system, councillors and officers will come under increasing pressure to add further funds to the annual base budget. Schools, of course, welcome this.

One particular area in which schools will make fortuitous underspendings is in the salaries of teachers. It is not possible, of course, to plan teacher movement, but when a teacher does move, the replacement is usually, but not always, on a lower incremental point in the salary scale. Historically, this salary drift means a reduction of approximately 2% in the total salary budget of an education authority or, put in another way, an additional 2% in the total number of teachers. The problem arises when attempting to apply this to individual schools. In smaller primary schools, for example, no teacher may leave over a period of ten years. These schools would find it very difficult to manage an annual 2% planned underspending in their teachers' salary budget.

With such detailed budgets being given to schools, much time is spent on dicussion over relatively trivial amounts. 'Should a school have either £170 or £180 for window cleaning?' is one that comes to mind. Such detailed discussion is an expensive waste of officers' and heads' time. Surely a simple solution is required. Paradoxically, the search for a simple solution will prove to be difficult. Cambridgeshire spent over a year in planning and consultation before arriving at a formula for distributing resources. The first attempt was based on the number of pupils in a school. It was discovered that, in secondary schools, the funding per pupil ranged from £850 a year in one school to £1270 in another. Variations are caused by factors such as the size of the school, the type of premises and positive discrimination by officers. Special needs, social class of the catchment area, split sites and turnover of pupils also needed to be taken into account. Another model was prepared, based on the organisation of the school. This model was eventually rejected by a majority of the Education Commit- tee who preferred the simplicity of an age-weighted pupil unit formula which is to be introduced into all secondary schools in 1988. Special pleading by individual schools will not be allowed for relatively minor budget headings such as advertising, interview expenses, examination expenses, capitation and car allowances. All these items will be included in the basic formula.

The use of premises by officers and advisers for meetings is another problem to be resolved. A Saturday course could cost a school £300 in heating bills alone. Such costs are not usually considered when planning courses. What is required is a central pool from which recharges to schools can be made. Such a cost accounting system would be efficient, need create little bureaucracy, and would make all concerned more aware of actual costs.

As governors and headteachers grow in confidence there will be an increasing number of requests to increase the amount of delegation. Such items as school meals, maintenance, school−crossing patrols and even debt charges will be raised. Schools will want to purchase the time of advisors and peripatetic music teachers. They will not be prepared to take a Scale 3 permanent unattached supply teacher for a Scale 1 allocation of money.

A major problem is the issue of redeployed teachers. Schools with falling rolls will receive reduced budgets, and will be quick to nominate teachers for deployment. Schools will also not be prepared to take expensive redeployed teachers. This will become even more difficult for LEAs if the Government gives schools increased powers in the appointment of teachers.

Community education

Schools can be the centre of much community activity. This is espe- cially true of the secondary school serving rural towns or the primary school in a village. It makes sense that the facilities available should be used by the whole community and not only by those of statutory school age. In the more enlightened authorities, schools are encouraged to become community schools with aims and objectives beyond that of a typical day school. Local Financial Management does not produce any problems for these schools – in fact it positively helps the community aspect to flourish. An additional budget is simply added to the school budget for use at the governors' discretion, providing that certain criteria are met. The real problem for Local Financial Management is when local education authorities have a policy of two or more institutions operating in one building. In such cases there is no clear senior manager of the building. In the day time the headteacher may try to economise on fuel, only to suspect that the adult education principal is wasting it in the evening. Of course, a true cost accounting system could be established but this would be expensive in administrative time. A fully integrated system is the only sensible approach. Under such a system, the caretaker is responsible to one person only; there is only one office, one resources centre, one furniture account, one account for lettings, etc. Another bonus is that a good community school will have a far better community development programme than a school with separate adult and youth programmes. A community programme will, of course, not isolate adults from youths, retired people from playgroups. Education is from the cradle to the grave and schools should not be separate from the community that they serve. Local Financial Management must eventually lead to the development of more and more community centres.

In many Authorities, however, there will be much resistance to this integrated approach. Opposition will come from some councillors, some officers and from staff involved solely in community education. Many staff will not want to be part of a community school and, indeed, may be prevented by lack of qualifications from joining such a school. They will argue that many people have developed a hostile view to school and will not take part in a community education programme if it is seen to be associated with a school. This is a sad and retrogressive approach, which helps to prevent some of the population realising the changing role of the modern community school.

Another fear is that the schools to which additional resources are given for community education will neglect those members of the community outside the statutory school age. Governing bodies of community schools may need, during their training sessions for LFM, to be reminded of their responsibilities as governors of the *whole* community school. They are not simply governors of a part of such a school. The authority, too, has a duty to monitor and to give clear guidelines to these governors.

Most authorities will allow their schools to be used free of charge for certain activities such as Scouts, Guides, playgroups, groups for the unemployed, WEA etc. Schools will want to ensure that they are given a budget to cover such activities. A true cost-accounting system will have to be developed and this can be used for other activities. Adult education centres using schools can be charged accordingly.

Cambridgeshire community schools have community associations with responsibility for setting fees for local affiliated groups. The county policy is that at least 20% of such fees must be given to the schools. Governors, under LFM, will want to ensure that these fees are not unrealistically low although they will want these affiliated groups to continue to use the premises. One solution may be for governors to ensure that they have representatives on the community association committee and for this committee to ensure that they have representatives on the governors' finance committee.

The full integration of community and school budgets in community schools has allowed an increasing number of teachers to become involved with community activities. In 1987, one Cambridgeshire community school altered its school day in order that the school timetable could be completed by 3.00pm. It then operates an extensive community programme from 3.00pm, encouraging school pupils to remain for a variety of activities. Teachers can receive additional payments under the community education programme as many adults and primary school children join these activities. Staff previously only associated with community education become full members of the school staff, with greatly improved career opportunities. At least two schools have recently appointed such staff to deputy head posts.

In conclusion, one must recommend the full community school approach with increased opportunities for both school pupils and all other members of the community. Local Financial Management will surely lead to the increased development of such schools.

Conclusions

Does Local Financial Management really improve the education service? All pilot results suggest that it does, but improvements may be simply the result of initial enthusiasm. Evaluation needs to be carried out over a long period. However, it is interesting to note some tentative conclusions:

1 After passing through a period of anxiety, the participants are pleased with their experience.

2 Headteachers report greater job satisfaction and welcome the additional responsibility.

3 Governors feel that they can become involved with their schools.

4 Teaching staffs have increased morale due to more resources becoming available.

5 Pupils take more care of their environment and respond academically.

6 A spirit of initiative is encouraged, increasing the will to work.

7 Decisions are made and jobs are done more quickly, leading to savings in time and energy.

Finally, Local Financial Management is a good principle and, as such, it has been welcomed by councillors, officers, governors, heads and parents.

Questions for discussion

1 *Do you agree with David Hill's assertion that LEAs have tended to underestimate the management potential of their heads?*

2 *What is your reaction to David Hill's suggestion that it is better to start with a small group of schools having a large budget area rather than all schools with a limited budget area? Discuss the pros and cons of both approaches.*

3 *If an 'implementation team' is to be used, can you detect ways in which administrative savings could be made at school or LEA level so that LFM does not bring about an overall increase in administrative costs?*

4 *Does David Hill convince you that there are going to be enough governors coming forward with the expertise and time to devote to LFM? What might be the implications for the recruitment of governors and do you think that there will be significant regional variations?*

5 *How does LFM affect the 'autocratic head'? Do you share the fears that LFM will make him/her worse? Do you see any ways in which LFM might be a lever to diminish the alleged autocracy of heads?*

6 *Looking at what David Hill refers to as the 'underfunding of the base budget' (page 105) do you see this as an argument against having a global formula such as advocated later in this article, and by Haydn Howard in Chapter 6 (page 114).*

7 *Do you fear the possibility of heads being reluctant to let schools be used out-of-hours unless there is a clear profit? What safeguards can you draw out of David Hill's article which might protect socially useful but commercially unprofitable activities?*

8 *Do you accept David Hill's argument that there is no realistic long-term alternative for community education except as part of an LFM system incorporating day-time and evening use? Some examples of possible areas of conflict are given; can you think of any others and can you devise strategies to overcome these problems in advance?*

9 *David Hill concludes with a message of encouragement. If you were trying to persuade your LEA to undertake LFM, in what order of priority would you list the perceived advantages?*

Chapter 6 The Finance Officer's perspective
Haydn Howard

Writing as an Assistant Director of Finance and Administration attached to the County Education Department, Haydn Howard looks at some of the technical financial aspects of LFM, while reaffirming that the scheme is principally about management rather than money. He looks at the way the budget is generated at the centre, how resources may be allocated to schools, how schools can then prepare their own budget and how expenditure can be controlled and he suggests measures by which the effectiveness of the scheme might be evaluated. He concludes with comments on the problem of central purchasing arrangements and on the position of a county treasurer when LFM is in operation.

The Cambridgeshire initiative has always stressed that the central philosophy underlying LFM is the devolution of decision making about a school's business to local managers. Obviously such delegation embraces processes and elements which are much more wide-ranging than simply finance. In retrospect there may have been more merit in calling the initiative 'local management' without any reference to finance. That title might have better captured or conveyed what the scheme is really concerned with.

Having said that, it is difficult to avoid the financial dimension at every turn. Good financial management and practice are absolutely fundamental to the success of the local management approach in schools . . . just as they are in any major undertaking. The budget of an average secondary school in Cambridgeshire is of the order of £1M. That is a substantial sum of money. Proper financial planning, control and discipline at local and central levels are essential for effective stewardship and management of such resources. But the point is that getting the financial matters right is a means to the end and not the end in itself.

The purpose of this chapter is to explore the financial issues and problems which are key to a scheme of management devolution to schools.

Budget generation

One important distinction must be clearly understood. There are two quite separate processes involved in the activity which is commonly referred to as budgeting. The first is the process of *generating* a budget, in the LFM context that means determining the total sum available to the scheme of local management. The second involves the *distribution* of that total sum to schools within the scheme in the authority.

The generation of the total sum available for spending in the forthcoming financial period will depend on an authority's perception of the appropriate balance between service needs and affordability. This process of generation is informed and influenced by a wide range of local and national pressures: the local demand for resources, the economic situation, government policy, political attitudes and so on. The reconciliation of all of these, mostly competing, factors leads eventually to the determination of a sum available for spending within the education service, and each of the phases within the service.

The outcome of an authority's budgetary deliberations may well not be known until just a few weeks before the start of the new financial period. This situation is most unhelpful to the process of local management but, sadly, is usually unavoidable.

The important point to recognise is that the product of the budget generation process is the definition of the total budgetary cake available for the service. The slicing of that cake is the process of distributing those available resources.

In most authorities the distinction between the two processes of generation and distribution is blurred by their approach to budgeting. Most authorities still adopt the time-honoured method whereby the previous year's base is incremented to take account of key variables – in particular, inflation and any growth planned by the authority.

With this traditional approach the pattern of resource distribution mirrors the means of budget generation. Indeed the anticipated pattern of distribution governs the generation of the budget. In other words the cake is sized to provide for the previous year's allocation of resources as updated for adjustments at the margin.

Authorities may adopt this approach at different levels. Some simply define a budget at phase level (say for all secondary schools), analysing planned expenditure over staffing, premises, equipment, supplies and sevices. Others extend this analysis down to the level of each individual school. But with the traditional approach the making of the cake and its slicing are largely determined by previous spending patterns and the system tends to preserve those patterns.

There are ways of generating a budget which are more sensitive to current needs. Some authorities already generate their budgets by reference to a particular rationale which gears resources to client needs in some structured way. The two most popular approaches are either to relate the planned inputs directly to pupil numbers or to generate a budget by reference to an agreed curriculum model. Again, the budget can be generated at a global level, ie for all secondary schools, or at the individual school level and then aggregated. Thereafter, the manner of distribution is likely to reflect the process of generation.

It certainly seems appropriate for the future that these more considered and structured approaches be used to generate a budget. Nonetheless the traditional approach can still be applied to generate a total fund available for the local management scheme. Traditional methods cannot, however, be effectively employed for the process of resource allocation, as shall be seen later.

It would be inappropriate to give local managers the whole of the budgetary cake generated by one of these mechanisms. Certain resources are less appropriate for local management than others. Some simply must be managed by the centre. The recent government consultation paper explored this issue and concluded that the following items should perhaps be excluded from local control:

1 Capital spending and associated debt charges, insurance;

2 Administration currently carried out by the LEA, including pay, tax and superannuation matters, accounts etc;

3 Provision of advisory and inspection services;

4 Provision of the education welfare service, education psychology service, school library service, and financial, legal and medical advice;

5 Supply cover for long-term staff absences, and redundancy payments where the need for redundancies is agreed between the LEA and the schools;

6 Expenditure supported by central government grants;

7 Home-to-school transport and pupil support;

8 (possibly) school meals.

It is gratifying to note that this accords almost exactly with the Cambridgeshire approach.

Maintenance of premises is a notable exception from the list. It is not clear what the Government would propose for this head of spending. In Cambridgeshire, planned maintenance is still in the hands of the Property Department. Schools have some control over breakdown maintenance. A pilot scheme of property bursars, whereby a local property officer manages the maintenance of a number of properties in an area in consultation with local managers, has been well received in Cambridgeshire and is favoured as a model for the future.

Resource allocation

At present, the approach to distributing resources to schools varies considerably between authorities. Some have sophisticated systems for allocating teachers and ancillary staff to schools, based on a rationale such as pupil numbers or a curriculum base. Further logic may be applied to distribute other provisions, especially capitation allowances.

Some authorities try to refine the process by making an initial allocation based upon some common denominator and then varying this basic allocation in the light of perceived local need. Such need may be measured in an objective way through the use of indices of local need. Often it is determined by 'professional judgement'.

Even though an allocation may be made to the school it is quite common to find that the same authority does not try to control expenditure at that level. It resorts instead to control at the aggregate (that is to say all schools) level.

Yet other authorities do not touch on the school level at all; their budgeting practice goes no further than determining a single account for all schools within a particular phase. They may lack the inclination, the resources or the systems to undertake an analysis of the overall sum available, school-by-school.

It will come as no surprise to hear that for local management to be credible, especially to local managers, there has to be a comprehensive, demonstrable and even-handed way of allocating available resources to schools. I strongly believe that such a system must also be simple to understand and to operate. Systems which may be called 'sophisticated' in seeking to reflect everyone's perception of slight deviation in local circumstances will be impossible to support in the longer term. They will give rise to a budgeting bureaucracy which will be expensive and inevitably inefficient. In any event local financial planning will be considerably enhanced if the school managers can readily understand the system of resource allocation.

One of the greatest challenges for authorities embarking on the process of devolving financial management is to identify a firm base, most likely a new base, for allocating resources to local management. Much allocation is still based on a traditional approach to budgeting whereby school budgets tend to be converted from year to year simply by incrementing the previous base to allow for inflation and marginal adjustments.

In my opinion an approach to resource allocation which relies on such traditional methods of budgeting is doomed to failure. One of the main reasons is that, under the traditional approach, the local manager considers that the allocation process is open to negotiation. Because the allocation is not derived from a clear and simple slicing process of a pre-determined cake, the local manager expects to enter into negotiation on each line of the budget. Central and local management, approaching the issue from their different standpoints, will inevitably differ in their views of what is a reasonable basis for determining the provision made for a school, in total and for each heading of expenditure. The arguments may well endure beyond the start of the spending year.

While using traditional methods for allocating resources in Cambridgeshire there has been considerable pressure to negotiate, particularly over the major spending heads. The discussions can also extend to more detailed issues. I even heard it argued by one headteacher that the allowance for interview expenses was inadequate because it did not take account of his school's distance from the railway station!

Every school regards its needs as being special and under the traditional approach to allocation the argument about a fair share of resources will never cease. An authority could not afford the time it would take to support such a system of negotiated settlement. It would be grossly inefficient.

A second important shortcoming of the traditional approach to resource allocation is that it usually requires a budget which has been created at a summary level, – say, for all secondary schools – to be disaggregated. In Cambridgeshire a budget of over £50M had to be broken down into 46 individual budgets for each secondary school. The problems involved in the process of disaggregation are manifold. The most significant issue is that when budgeting at the summary level a number of assumptions can be quite properly applied. These will include, for instance, an allowance for staff turnover; it is inevitable that during the course of a year, savings will be made on account of some staff leaving and others starting. The new starter often commences at a lower rate of pay and a temporary vacancy may occur before the newcomer takes up post. This effects savings and it is right and proper that a corresponding reduction be made in fixing the overall budget.

Such adjustments, however, are less easy to justify when budgeting at the level of the individual school. The pattern of turnover differs markedly from one school to another. The local manager, not surprisingly, becomes suspicious and resists any attempt to reduce the school's budgetary provision. And yet without these reductions, the budget is, in global terms, overprovided and overgenerous.

A further shortcoming of traditional budgeting is that it is often unfair. There is a tendency for extra resources to be allocated to an individual school to satisfy perceived need, usually on a subjective basis and at a particular point in time. Those resources often then become built into the base budget of the school. Subsequently, when the cost per pupil of two esssentially similar schools is compared, there can be substantial discrepancies.

The key to success is a simple and robust means of distributing the total available resources by way of formula, a structured approach to distribution which can be readily expressed. It could be that the general formula embraces a number of 'sub-formulas'. In other words:

$$A \text{ could equal } B + C + D. \ldots$$

where B, C, D. . . . are derived by separate self-contained formulas.

It is essential however that the formula can be easily understood. It seems inevitable that any formula must be related essentially to pupil numbers and/or to curriculum or organisational bases.

The principle behind formula allocation is quite simply to allocate the lion's share of the budget available to the scheme of local management on a pro-rata basis to each school. Some have argued for a raw allocation, that is to say a simple slicing according to formula factors with no adjustment or refinement. Such an approach, however, is likely to create considerable losses and gains for individual schools by comparison with current levels of resources. There is a need, therefore, for some form of protection. This can be achieved in part by allocating certain funds directly to individual schools *before* applying the pro-rata approach.

There are several sums which could be allocated directly:

1   BASIC CASH GRANT

A minimum cash grant could be allocated to all schools. This would help to protect the small schools which have tended to be favoured by the traditional approach to allocating resources.

2 PREMISES-RELATED COSTS

There is a strong case for allocating some of the resources by reference to historical budget allocations. Certain areas of spending in a school bear little direct relation to pupil numbers or curriculum activities. This is particularly true of premises-related costs such as:

- fuel
- caretaking and cleaning
- general rates
- water and sewerage charges
- window cleaning

These provisions could be allocated directly to schools on the basis of historical costs.

3 NATIONAL GRANTS

The appropriate sum from national grants could be allocated directly to each school for:

- TVEI
- ESGs for midday supervision, GCSE, INSET
- Section 11

4 REORGANISATION AND REVIEW

The cost implications of decisions of the authority concerning schools' reorganisation and review may be recompensed by allocating directly to eligible schools sums to fund the ongoing expense of, for instance, protected salaries. Cambridgeshire proposes to allocate 0.33% of the budget in this way.

5 SPECIAL FACTORS

Account could be taken of perceived local (and significant) needs of each school by allocating funds directly on account of certain factors such as a relative poverty factor (say of the order of 1% of the total budget) perhaps related to numbers eligible for free school meals; or a relative pupil turnover factor, perhaps 0.5% of the total budget.

Once such sums had been allocated directly, a balance would remain for allocation of funds on a pro-rata basis for:

- teachers
- supply teachers
- foreign language assistants
- support staff
- supplies and materials

- examinations
- car allowances
- advertising
- interview expenses

Cambridgeshire has given detailed consideration to two different approaches to distributing the balance of funds by way of formula factors. One approach applies the Age Weighted Pupil Unit (AWPU) whilst the other uses Organisation Based Staffing (OBS).

Age Weighted Pupil Unit (AWPU)

The essence of this approach is to allocate resources in relation to the pupil population in each school, but using an age weighting to vary the resource entitlement of particular age groups. It is a practice which is well established in the education service. The particular weightings presently contemplated by the Cambridgeshire system are:

Age group	Unit
Years 1 to 3	1
Years 4 to 5	20/16
Years 6+	20/11

There has been much discussion on the appropriateness of the units for the various age groups. One of the attractions of the approach is its simplicity. It would be an easy matter to vary the units from time to time.

Organisation Based Staffing (OBS)

The AWPU approach takes broad account of the composition of the school population. But it is not sensitive to the implications, especially for the teaching resource, of the distribution of population within a school by each individual year group. The organisation based staffing (OBS) approach attempts to be sympathetic to this issue. It would allocate funds by a financial model of organisation based staff, using assumptions of how the grouping of pupils in a notional school of any particular size could be organised.

Suggested assumptions are:

1 Basic calculations derived from:

Age group	Periods	Max class size
Yrs 1,2,3	36	27
	4	20

Yrs 4,5	32	24
	8	20
Yrs 6,7	32	Teacher staffing 1 to 12

2 Additional calculations based on:

- a teaching contact ratio of 0.8 for Yrs 1 to 5
- 5% for special needs
- small year groups:

Age group	No of pupils	Additional periods per year
Yrs 1,2,3	up to 99	4
Yrs 4,5	up to 95	12
Yrs 4,5	96–119	4

The two formula variants, AWPU and OBS, need not be mutually exclusive. Cambridgeshire has recently introduced a refinement to its AWPU approach which is based on OBS concepts. This is an organisation factor which is related to the size of the age group entering and moving through the school. It recognises the organisational issues of the 'smaller' school. Before applying AWPU for slicing, 1.8% of the budget would be shared between schools of five forms of entry and below, on a graduated scale. A further 0.2% of the total budget would be allocated to the two sixth form colleges.

Despite the elements of protection outlined above, a number of schools are still likely to lose significant amounts of resource through use of the formula allocation. Most schools must, in any case, manage cash reductions because of falling rolls. The transition to formula will add to these losses in some schools. The formula approach proposed in Cambridgeshire does not distinguish between losses on account of formula and losses due to falling rolls.

To mitigate resource reductions in schools, a further level of protection is favoured in Cambridgeshire, that is, to phase the impact of any revised method of allocation over time. This simply means that losses and gains will be reduced in the early years to ease the transition. Any loss or gain at school level will be halved and then limited to a maximum change of 5% compared with the school's allocation in the previous year.

Incidentally, there is further scope for protection by using an earlier time basis (eg the previous January) for pupil numbers. This would favour schools with falling rolls.

The resultant formula may be simply expressed as:

$$\text{School allocation} = \text{Direct allocations} + \frac{\text{Remainder}}{\text{AWPU or OBS}} \pm \text{phasing factor}$$

Cambridgeshire's Education Committee has chosen the AWPU approach for allocating resources to all secondary schools in the financial year 1988–89. The Committee liked the concept of the OBS approach but felt it was more appropriate for generating a budget and preferred the simplicity of the AWPU method for allocating resources.

Budget preparation

Under LFM budget preparation becomes a task to be undertaken by the local manager within the total sum allocated to the school by the allocation process. This is not to be confused with the process of budget generation which is undertaken at the centre. What we are concerned with here is the preparation of the spending plan for the school for the next financial period.

It is normally a fresh experience for the school manager to need to prepare the budget for most of the resources within and around the school. He or she will, however, have had extensive experience of managing the likes of capitation allowances and will already well understand the tenets of financial management. It is vital, nevertheless, that strong support is given from the centre towards the process of budget preparation.

It may be that in the early stages the local manager wishes to abide by an existing base budget for the school (assuming that such exists). As long as this spending plan fits within the school's allocation it is reasonable to do so. Indeed it should not be assumed that all local managers approach the budget preparation with a clean sheet. In Cambridgeshire, most financial plans tend to be derived by adjusting a previous base at the margins. This can prove to be a safe and secure approach as long as the product provides a credible plan for the period. But obviously the culture of local financial management is for the school manager to prepare financial plans within available resources which more ably match local needs and circumstances. This will only be achieved by a structured and informed reconciliation of requirements with resources.

There are two important refinements to budget management which Cambridgeshire has practised. First, the sum allocated to a school is regarded as a cash limit and the local manager is free to prepare the school budget within that overall figure. Naturally, the manager will need assistance in the early years if such freedom is to be much exercised. It is all too easy for a plan that looks sound in theory to the local observer to lead to problems in practice.

To ease the budgetary task, the local manager is permitted to transfer sums from one budget heading to another after the start of the budget year. This practice is known as virement. In theory virement could entail the movement of large sums of money. In practice the sums transferred are modest, so that the facility is used for fine tuning and not for major alteration to a budget.

The second important initiative is the carry-forward facility. Under the Cambridgeshire system, local managers are allowed to carry forward, albeit within certain limits, overspendings and underspendings into the next financial period. This eases the burden of getting everything absolutely right at the outset but again the facility must be used with extreme caution.

Control monitoring

It seems almost too obvious to say that there is a critical need for competent budgetary control, that is to say the process of managing actual expenditure to keep it in line with the budget plan. Naturally this process will be eased if the original budget is soundly based and accurately reflects the resource requirements of the school within the limits set. However, throughout the budget period changes will occur. The need to spend is likely to differ from pre-set levels. New pressures will appear and changes will need to be made to the planned pattern of spending.

There are, of course, two levels of control which need to be considered – the central level and the local school level. The crucial aspect of financial devolution is that, by definition, control over spending has been passed down to the local level. This means that at the centre there is considerably less scope for influencing the course of spending. This gives rise to a feeling of lack of control over total cash spending by the centre. The problem is intensified when schools are allowed the facility to carry forward underspendings or overspendings into a subsequent budget period. Under the recent regime of grant penalties for excess spending, the centre runs the risk of facilitating a general unplanned overspending if all schools were to exceed their budget allocations in a particular period. The consequences of any unplanned overspending would be unpleasant, to say the least.

Another factor is that once the total budget for schools has been allocated to the individual management units, there is nothing left to allow scope for manoeuvre at the centre. There is no money to respond to sudden unexpected pressures. This argues strongly for the creation of a holdback or a reserve fund, amounting to perhaps 1% of the budget, which may be held centrally to fund unforeseen needs. But this is not likely to be well received by local managers since, quite obviously, any sum reserved at the centre reduces the amount available for distribution.

The tools for controlling expenditure at the centre remain much the same. The centre will have the same level of information about spending as it did before devolution. The task simply becomes harder because control has been moved down to the local level. The main task at the centre is to spot significant deviation in particular schools at an early stage, since this may indicate a lack of local control. Care must be taken, however, in following up any indicators since the local manager may be quite properly exercising local discretion. Some tolerance factor needs to be set, beyond which preliminary investigation is triggered. This could be set at a level of, say, 3–5% deviation from planned spending.

It is at the local level that the process of control is now most keenly felt. It calls for substantial commitment to constant monitoring of expenditure against pre-set limits. The management functions for achieving this are simply defined. However, their execution depends very much on the quality of the financial systems which are employed to provide the information and the skills which managers demonstrate in acting upon that information.

There can be no substitute for extensive use of technology at both the centre and local level in order to capture and to manage the requisite information. There is also a need for a reliable interface between information kept at central and local levels. It will be a long time (if ever) before the likes of the payroll function can be performed at the local level. Until such time the school is dependent on the central systems for the supply of information concerning payments to staff. It is vital that this information is communicated promptly and accurately to schools. There is, however, ample scope for much of the other information about expenditure on supplies, equipment and services to be sourced and managed at the local level and maintained on a commitment basis (rather than the cash spent basis of the centre). Such a local facility for recording commitments for comparison with budgeted levels is essential for the proper management of funds.

It is extremely unlikely, in view of the numbers of transactions inherent in such a system, that a support function could be operated effectively on a manual basis. The average turnover of a secondary school is likely to be of the order of £1M per annum. Control of spending of this dimension requires capable systems.

Some will argue that the proper place for storing this information will be on the authority's mainframe computer. Given sufficient resources, skills and expertise, this could probably be achieved, but it would need very careful consideration of the implications of the kind of service which the local manager requires. With LFM the local manager is entitled to define the school's financial information needs and to expect an accurate and timely response. Experience shows that the level of detail required by the local manager will put a strain on all but the most powerful and versatile of central systems. By comparison a local microcomputer system – with a friendly face – seems to have much to commend it.

Having said that, we must not lose sight of the need for a proper reconciliation of the books in the school with those of the centre. Whatever the local records say at school level, it is the central mainframe records which constitute the books of the authority. There must be a sound and demonstrable reconciliation between the two sets of records.

Measuring/evaluating

The process of measuring and evaluating is critical to all aspects of local management in schools and particularly to the financial dimension. It is not sufficient simply to audit the propriety which has been exercised in the stewardship of funds. There must also be a measure of the effectiveness of local management decisions. It is all too easy, under the scheme of local management, for money to be reapplied in new or different ways. Care must be taken in measuring performance to ensure that short-term benefit has not been pursued at the expense of longer-term integrity. A simple example of this is the local manager who may spend large amounts on consumable supplies within the period and thereby much impress the local audience in the short term. But such spending may well have been facilitated by reduced investment in, say, furniture and equipment. Over a few short years the school inventory could be seriously depleted. Prudent financial management must take account of the long as well as the short term.

There is clearly a role for the authority's internal audit team in this process of evaluation. In many authorities there will need to be a reorientation away from the traditional petty cash audit approach in schools towards a methodology for evaluating the efficiency and effectiveness of local financial management.

This is easier said than done. It requires reliable performance indicators and many have sought in vain for an appropriate portfolio. However, the fact that the tools for measuring may be imperfect should not be used as an excuse for deferring the process. There is sufficient material and know-how to make a credible, if perhaps modest, start towards performance measurement.

Reasonable measures of performance are available in the areas of heating and cleaning. Property departments should be able to offer reliable indicators of efficiency and effectiveness of operation which take account of variations in local property factors, such as heating plant and insulation, and external factors such as temperature. It may be that fuel budgets for individual establishments can be generated on the basis of such information. Similarly, with cleaning, standard times and costs for cleaning various types of accommodation are usually readily available to serve as a basis for performance measurement.

In other spending areas, especially in the case of staffing and curriculum outputs, the task is obviously more difficult. Finite measures are notoriously difficult to secure. There is ample scope, however, for comparative measures to be made, particularly over time. Much can be done to measure improvements in a school's performance from year to year by evaluating factors as diverse as examination results, success in placing students for further study or work, condition and sufficiency of furnishings, equipment and materials, and parental opinion (maybe only expressed through choice of school).

Central purchasing

One particular concern which often surfaces in discussions relates to the implications of LFM for central purchasing. Some authorities feel concerned that delegation might blunt purchasing efficiency. On the other hand, local managers often see central purchasing as a straitjacket to procurement.

The underlying aim of local financial management is fully compatible with that of central purchasing; to achieve a more effective use of resources. Cambridgeshire, like all authorities, has a well developed central purchasing function, yet it co-exists with the LFM scheme. The central expertise continues to be keenly applied in the negotiation of contract prices for the supply of goods and services. Schools determine and independently order their own selection and quantity of goods. Any just cause for deviating from these purchasing arrangements would be contemplated, but the need has not yet been strongly voiced.

It is interesting to note that prior to LFM there was little comment about prevailing contract prices for commodities. Since its introduction there has been much comment that some prices could be bettered. It may be that, on occasion, this is so. The argument is well known in central purchasing circles. There will always be opportunities for some cheaper purchases to be made outside negotiated contracts. The critical test is whether better prices can be secured and *maintained* for most commodities by the local manager or, alternatively, whether local purchasing of cheaper items on a small scale would not prejudice the rest of the negotiated contracts and prices. Otherwise there is a danger of throwing away the wider scale benefits of central purchasing in return for a small local gain.

Sadly, central purchasing does seem to fall down regularly on matters of procedure. Systems seem to be universally complicated, slow to inform and inaccurate, leaving the local manager to reconcile, with difficulty, items requisitioned against items delivered or charged. Streamlining of the process would do much to ease the workload and enhance the confidence of local management.

A popular topic of discussion about LFM is the case for giving control of the cheque book to the local manager. Headteachers put forward eloquent arguments in support of such a facility. Perhaps the most compelling is that giving the bank account and the cheque book to the local manager is a logical extension of local financial management. It seems to capture the spirit of financial delegation. Headteachers offer anecdotal evidence that quicker payment of invoices can secure better prices, especially if a cheque can be drawn at the time of delivery. There could be an easier reconciliation of cash with spending if the cheque book was controlled locally. The problem which the local manager has in reconciling his analysis of spending with the relevant bank statement is likely to be easier if that account is directly under his control.

There are, however, very potent arguments against local bank accounts. The most convincing is the likely loss of interest earnings to the authority. Local authorities play a very efficient money lending game with funds in hand pending their disbursement. If funds equating to the schools' budget were divided between many bank accounts then interest earnings would be much harder to sustain. Headteachers say that they could earn interest by placing their local funds on deposit. It's not as simple as that. The demands of cash flow require a reasonable balance to be kept in the current account. And once the funds have been divided up between 50 or so school bank accounts, the scope which the authority had for lending the aggregated sum on a short term basis, such as overnight, is lost. Small sums are not attractive to the money broker or borrower.

Another important consideration is that, where cash is involved, there is a need for a high audit profile. The use of local cheque books would create a significant demand for extra audit resources. Not only would this add to the burden at the centre but it would also impact upon the schools, since they would have to facilitate the auditing process.

A further factor is that many cheques would be sent to regular suppliers instead of only a few, as happens under the central methods of payment. This could affect purchasing contracts with suppliers if there was a significant increase in their administrative load. The notion of local cheque books is alluring, but such an initiative could be costly in practice.

The treasurer's control

There will, inevitably, be some concern among treasurers about financial control being passed down into the hands of local school managers. The degree of concern will differ between authorities, depending on their management style. Some may see it as a loss of power. Such concern is not as sharply felt within Cambridgeshire since the concept of LFM fits neatly within the Council's corporate culture of enabling the fullest delegation consistent with effectiveness. Moreover, heads are recognised as highly competent managers. As such they share in the very progressive training facilities which are available to senior managers within the authority. Heads are regarded as an integral part of the senior management structure of the authority. It does not feel odd, therefore, to entrust to them the financial function which, after all, is a key and integral management responsibility.

Naturally, the treasurer has to ensure that safe and efficient arrangements are implemented and maintained for the stewardship of schools' funds which are under local control. There is ample scope for realising that objective, especially given the opportunity afforded by technology for facilitating the necessary safeguards. Inevitably, however, there will be a significant increase in the need for auditing effort and skills.

In less enlightened environments there will, no doubt, be concern about the potential loss of power or control at the centre. The Cambridgeshire experience has been that the process of financial management is strengthened by the participation of the local manager. Heads take their financial responsibilities seriously and make a substantial contribution to better informing the processes of budget generation, resource allocation and financial control.

It must be said, however, that LFM has emerged from a particular corporate culture and management style. Whether such an initiative can be imposed successfully on LEAs of widely differing complexions remains to be seen.

Another concern often expressed by local managers focuses on what happens if an error is made in the local budget by the LEA . . . who pays? It has to be accepted that LFM must operate in the real world. Mistakes will happen. Who pays for them should perhaps depend on who was party to making the mistakes in the first place. Under LFM, the local manager usually has access to as much information as the centre.

It must also be appreciated that if all the budget is allocated out to individual schools then there is no scope at the centre for meeting the costs of correcting errors which emerge during the year. This may be viewed as a good reason for holding back some funds as a contingency for the unexpected. Less would then be available for distribution, and claims against the fund would be encouraged.

It is also noteworthy that the notion of errors is more likely to emerge under traditional budgeting. There is more scope for local managers to argue about particular allocations and their accuracy. If a lump sum is allocated to schools the scope for error is reduced since the local manager takes decisions on spending patterns. If an error was made in the initial allocation to the school, then the fault would seem to lie with the centre and it would be for them to correct.

There may be times when a reduction in spending is called for. This may emerge as part of a general council cut-back which could conceivably happen mid-year. In such cases local management cannot expect to avoid the situation. LFM is an integral part of the whole organisation.

Some occurrences which local managers tend to describe as errors are in fact difficult to categorise. A good example is an incorrect assessment of a teacher's salary which only comes to light after a number of years. This may be because, at the time of assessment, certain information was either not available or not known. Who pays the backpay, which can cost several thousands of pounds, the centre or the school? It is difficult to generalise; it depends on the circumstances of the case. In most instances, however, I would need to be persuaded that the local manager should not carry the costs. It is the school which determines who to appoint, and the school should, therefore, be aware of the implications of the cost of appointment. If information is not available at the time of appointment, then can the centre be solely to blame? If a simple mistake has been made by the centre in the payment process, then surely this should be picked up quickly at the school end.

I said at the beginning of this chapter that the financial dimension is a means to an end and not the end in itself. This is unquestionably so. Financial management is about helping to secure the aims of the organisation through efficiency and effectiveness. This chapter has sought to identify the key financial issues which surround the concept of local management. It is vital for its success that these issues are addressed and appropriately resolved. For, although financial management remains the means, skilful practices will inevitably deliver a much better end.

Questions for discussion

1 *Look again at the list of exclusions on page 113. In the light of what you have read since exclusions were first discussed in Part One, would you now wish to see some of these headings included in LFM? If so, which – and why? If not, why not?*

2 *Do you have any sympathy for the head with a school a long way from a railway station? Can you think of other local factors which might work against certain schools if resources were distributed on a crude formula?*

3 *The two main criticisms levelled against traditional budgeting are administrative inefficiency and operational inequity. Which do you think has been uppermost in convincing the Cambridgeshire members to opt for formula budgeting and why?*

4 *Divide the discussion group into AWPU and OBS factions. Let each group present their case concisely and then let them try to persuade each other of the strength of their own position. Do you think the differences embody significant issues of principle?*

5 *Do you accept the validity of any of the performance measures suggested on page 124? What others would you like to put forward in addition to, or instead of, those suggested?*

6 *Discuss the view that central purchasing and LFM are a fundamental contradiction.*

7 *What advantages would you see in having a cheque-book system for capitation expenditure?*

Chapter 7 The impact of LFM on a Local Education Authority

Tyrrell Burgess

In considering the distribution of funds by a local education authority, Tyrrell Burgess develops the argument for a 'simple solution' already touched on in the preceding chapter. He goes on to argue for new structures within an LEA and suggests ways in which the inspectorate should advise teachers and monitor schools' performance while handing over to schools, as well as the management of the budget, the development of their own solutions to their problems.

The power for rational improvement in schools which is offered by Local Financial Management is very great. The power for rational improvement in local education authorities is even greater. It can help them to make sensible decisions, not just about finance, but also about organisation and policy. In Cambridgeshire the consequences for schools are beginning to be clear, the consequences for the authority scarcely explored. Elsewhere the assumption seems to be that, as with most innovation, everything will go on much as before. It would be a pity if the chance for change were missed.

On finance the main problem seems almost technical: how to marry the new budgeting responsibilities of the schools with the generation of estimates by the authority. If properly solved, however, this can transform the knowledge and thought on which estimates are based, giving the authority better means to perform its statutory duties and thus more confidence to tackle its local educational problems. Improvements in policy and organisation will flow from this – if an authority accepts the implications of local financial management (and other changes, like the 'opting out' of schools from LEA maintenance) and reforms its structure and procedures to accommodate it.

School budgets and the distribution of funds

An authority which introduces local financial management will quickly come to see that if each school is to make its own budget and manage in line with this, then some way must be found of making this responsibility compatible with the authority's own creation of estimates and in particular with its own 'budget cycle' in the financial year. There are a number of ways of doing this, but the one chosen must have four characteristics. It must preserve and enhance the financial self-management of schools; maintain the authority's overall control of spending; improve the authority's own budgeting and be applicable to all schools. There are three obvious methods which meet these requirements to differing degrees: the 'integrated', the 'historical' and the 'independent'.

The *integrated* procedure was the one generally envisaged at the time of the 1944 Education Act. It was incorporated in the model articles of government issued by the then Ministry of Education and still appears in the articles of most secondary schools. Under such a scheme each school would have the initiative to submit estimates for the next financial year, early in the authority's budgeting process, so that these estimates could be considered by the authority and included in its own. Apparently this system did apply in practice in some authorities before 1974. Each school would in effect be making a 'bid' for a level of expenditure for the coming year and the authority would be involved in making a judgment on these bids. The schools and the authority would have an annual argument about finance. Such a scheme would recognise the financial self-management of schools, and indeed be based upon it, but it would cause a duplication of work, because the authority would have to have a basis for judging the schools' 'bids'. Its overall control would be vulnerable to pressure during the negotiations. In present circumstances, where governments create annual uncertainty in local government finance, the system would probably prove too complex and time-consuming. There is also a difficulty over presentation: the scheme would be damaged if teachers in schools suspected that the annual negotiations were designed to bring the fruits of efficiency and savings to the authority rather than to the schools themselves.

Under the *historical* method, which is employed by many authorities, an authority would build up its own budget as an aggregate of the budgets for each separate secondary school, in the light of historical and existing circumstances, known policies and other developments, and inflation. This has frequently been combined with an element of discretion for the schools themselves in expenditures under a 'capitation' allowance. This method, too, involves a duplication of work and would be found (as it was in Cambridgeshire pilot scheme) to provoke argument about whether the individual budgets built up in this way were apt for particular schools. Moreover, the strong implication of this method is that the school's responsibility is simply to administer budgetary decisions made elsewhere, not to make its own decisions to suit its own unique circumstances. If financial management is to be genuinely local, the schools must create their budgets as well as managing them.

An *independent* procedure would be one in which the authority's budget and the schools' budgets were separately determined. Under such a scheme the authority would determine the amount available to each school and make, as it were, a general grant to the school to spend as it wished. The schools would then budget within the given sum. Such a scheme would enable the detailed budgeting for individual schools to be done once only – within the schools themselves. It would enable the authority to simplify the ways by which it allocated funds to schools. It would give the schools more confidence that efficiency would be rewarded, because the schools would be responsible for determining their expenditures within a limit which had already been set. To gain the most benefit from such a scheme, the authority's determination of the total sums available for each school would be a matter of formulae and convention, rather than decisions on line-by-line estimates.

It has always seemed to me clear that the third of these, the independent method, is the most apt for Local Financial Management, and I recommended this (as external assessor to the Cambridgeshire project) in 1982. I did so for four main reasons. First, this method was the most consistent with the overall objects of Local Financial Management. It was recognised that exercising virement on a budget drawn up by offficers was qualitatively different from a school's drawing up and managing its own budget. In the first case the school would be merely reacting to external events, in the second the budget would become a powerful tool of management for the school itself. Second, experience suggested that assumptions which might be valid and defensible for the budget as a whole might become unrealistic when applied to individual schools. Third, the alternative method would perpetuate dispute between individual schools and the authority about the validity of the budgets. This would be exacerbated by suspicion in the schools that their good management in one year might be penalised in the budgets for succeeding years. Fourth, the chosen method would improve the authority's overall budgeting, in that information about the schools' practices would be flowing upwards from the schools rather than downwards from the 'office'. The independent method implied the separation of three functions. The first was the overall method of budgeting to be adopted by the authority. The second was the distributions within that overall budget, to individual schools. The third was the budgeting by the schools themselves.

Of these it is the distribution to schools that is the most critical for the success of Local Financial Management. An authority's capacity to generate estimates is not in question, though it can always be improved – and such improvements are considered later. The capacity of schools to create their own budgets has been widely regarded as problematic, but experience in Cambridgeshire has suggested that this capacity can quickly be developed, and without stress, provided the authority puts itself in a position to respond promptly to calls for information, explanation and advice. (In this respect, the work of the LFM team of officers in Cambridgeshire, as the scheme was generalised, was exemplary.)

The distributional problem is much less familiar. Briefly, it is to find a way of giving the schools their annual allocation without implying decisions about spending and thus inhibiting or even undermining their Local Financial Management. The obvious solution is to distribute a lump sum to each school, representing its share of the authority's total budget. But how is that sum to be arrived at?

Three possibilities come to mind. The first is a variation of the authority's own budgeting process applied to individual schools: it takes the current distribution as given and makes allowance for inflation, agreed improvement, economies and so on. The objection to this is that it reintroduces the bugbear of annual argument and is based too largely on past decisions which may or may not still be apt. A second method would take account of the authority's 'policy' – for example on the number of teachers and ancillaries needed. This also would give grounds for dispute. Moreover, it opens the prospect of limitless complexity as an authority tries to take account of numbers of different 'needs'.

My own preference was and is for the simplest possible formula, a distribution per pupil. This was the solution adopted in Cambridgeshire, though with modifications. The most important of these was to 'weight' the crude numbers to reflect existing staffing formulae for pupils of different ages. Another was the exclusion of certain items over which the school has little or no control. A third was a set of protective devices to ease the transition to the new system. (It must be said that the readiness of officers in Cambridgeshire to produce 'exemplifications' of the consequences to individual schools of different formulae was critical to the establishment of the scheme.)

The arguments for a per capita distribution are to my mind overwhelming. The method is immediately comprehensible, to schools and the public. It is open and predictable in its consequences. It accords with the logic of Local Financial Management and gives the greatest scope for local decision. Distributing money according to the numbers of pupils actually in the schools encourages the schools to think of meeting the requirements of those pupils directly rather than on the basis of historic or externally prescribed solutions.

Unfortunately this view is not yet widely accepted; the general propensity of human beings to get into a muddle is still strong. The threat to simplicity, rationality and elegance comes, as usual, from the well-meaning, both in authorities and in the schools themselves. On the one hand councillors and officers want any distributional formula to reflect policy; on the other, the schools want it to reflect organisation and curriculum. Both are asking the formula to do something it cannot, even in principle, do. The point is well illustrated by the Cambridgeshire experience. As the notion of a formula distribution became more familiar and acceptable, officers came under pressure from teacher representatives (to which some of their colleagues and councillors were sympathetic) to develop a formula based not on (weighted) pupil numbers, but on school organisation. Broadly this rested on assumptions about the curriculum and class sizes and the staffing needed to support them in schools of different sizes. The method seemed plausible because officers were already working on something similar as a means of adding rationality to the generation of the secondary school estimates as a whole. In the event, the authority decided against it, in favour of age-weighted pupil numbers.

The argument was worth having, however, because a number of things became clearer in the course of it. One was the value of simplicity and openness. Another was the unlikelihood of a general formula being apt for individual schools: for example, one might assume, for the purpose of preparing overall estimates, an annual turnover of teachers of 1½%; but an individual school might have no turnover at all, or twice the assumed rate or anything. A general formula, though said to be based on needs, cannot be based on the actual needs of any individual school, but only on the *notional* needs of schools as a class. A general formula to meet individual needs is a contradiction in terms. Moreover, if schools were in some sense required to operate according to the formula, it would frustrate their own Local Financial Management: if they were not, the formula was otiose. Above all, the argument raised serious questions both about the nature of 'policy' in a local authority and the means by which it might be implemented, questions that are considered below (pp 142).

In seeking to generalise Local Financial Management, the Government has made clear that authorities will need to propose some formula for distributing resources to individual schools. If reports are correct, its first thoughts are tending towards the complex needs-based or policy-based variety. It will be for the more intelligent local authorities to show a better way.

The authority's estimates

It is not just in distribution that openness and simplicity are important: with Local Financial Management they can inform all an authority's financial processes. At present the generation of estimates is extremely complex, involving a number of different elements. These reflect, for example, an authority's committee structure (schools, further education), the budgets for individual schools and the overall budget headings (staffing, heating and lighting, equipment). Very broadly the estimate accommodates maintaining the service at the present level (given inflation), the consequences of developments already in hand and new developments which have been decided or may be decided during the coming year. Decisions at the various levels interact, and the consequence is a detailed set of estimates backed by work in even greater detail.

The purpose of the estimates is twofold: the first is to provide an indication of spending proposed for the coming year, so that the authority may set its rate, determine rents, fees and charges and attract the appropriate government grants. The second is to provide the basis for financial control. One implication of Local Financial Management is that this control will be exercised at the level of the school: an authority will no longer have control at the level of headings of expenditure. As the year goes by the authority will need to see that the aggregated spending of schools is not running above the estimate, and not running too far below it either. It will be possible for the authority to notice how far spending under detailed heads differs from the original estimate, but it will not be exercising control over this on a day to day basis. Nor will there be any point in building up estimates in any detail. The detail, if required, will be provided by the aggregate (under headings) of the school's individual estimates. This means that the authority's estimating can be done on the simplest and broadest basis, reflecting its general decisions on educational provision. Some examples may make this clear.

The major spending in education is on salaries, particularly the salaries of teachers. Here an authority needs to determine (on the basis of past experience and what it increasingly knows of the schools' needs and practice under Local Financial Management) what it regards as an acceptable overall staff-student ratio – let us say 1 to 16 in secondary schools and 1 to 22 in primary schools. It will know the average cost of a teacher and how many teachers are implied by its staff-student ratio for the number of children known to be in the schools. The overall estimate for teaching staff is readily and rapidly determined. Of course, on the basis of experience, and in the light of external circumstances, the authority may decide to improve or worsen the overall staff-student ratio: the decision may change but the process will remain the same. Under Local Financial Managment, the authority is likely to have a much richer understanding of the consequences of such a decision that it has ever had before, because it will understand how individual schools in fact use the resources available to them.

A similar kind of overall provision can be made for administrative and other ancillary staff. The authority might begin, on the basis of experience, by assuming an overall provision of secretarial and administrative staff, relating this to the number of students. A new development, like the introduction of GCSE, might suggest enhanced provision overall in secondary schools: this can quickly be reflected in the estimates.

Estimates for staff can readily be seen to be related to numbers of students. Estimates for such things as fuel and rates are generally thought to be related more to premises than to students. But it is important to remember that the task of the authority is to estimate its own (overall) expenditures, not the detailed expenditure of individual schools. On fuel, for example, it knows its overall bills from past experience. It can estimate movements in costs. Thus the generation of an overall fuel estimate is not difficult.

One question which is often raised by members of the authority is the way in which new 'policies' are reflected in the estimates. It depends on what the policies are and what resources they are thought to require. An argument to make greater provision for 'special needs', requiring additional teaching resources, should be reflected in the general decision about staffing ratios and thus in the staffing estimates. A policy to enhance the provision of textbooks and equipment in order to accommodate GCSE, for example, will be reflected in the capitation-based estimates for books and materials. A desire to 'protect' the curriculum in time of falling rolls will imply that staffing levels fall more slowly than student numbers; the current improvement in staffing ratios will again be reflected in the staffing estimates. And so on.

Similarly, the pressure from schools and others for improvement will be accepted or resisted by the authority in terms of its overall estimates.

In short, with Local Financial Management, the estimating process of the authority can be simple and swift. The detail is a matter for the schools. Because this is so, the knowledge which the authority has of what the schools think they require will be greatly enhanced. Financial control will be based in the schools, not in the detail of headings of estimates (where it was in any case always somewhat unreal).

Organisation and structure

It is at this point that experienced councillors and officers in local education authorities may wonder whether control has been not so much re-located as largely lost – at any rate to the authority. Wherein lies responsibility for the outcomes of these expenditures? What of quality and effectiveness? What has become of the authority's capacity to formulate and implement 'policy'? For what, if anything, are members to be accountable? These are all serious questions, and it is an advantage of Local Financial Management that it raises them in an acute form. It is my view that the general introduction of Local Financial Management offers an opportunity to reform the functions and structure of the local education authority itself.

The existing structures of a typical authority have simply grown over time. They contain features which have outlived their usefulness or which are not apt for new conditions. There is also continuing pressure for efficiency and savings in administration. The Chief Education Officer and his department have two main functions: to serve the authority and to serve the schools and other institutions. As an administration it is concerned with policy, control and supply.

These functions may be exercised through three or four separate forms of organisation, which may or may not be compatible with the way the members are organised in committees. One form of organisation is that of the 'service' divisions, like finance, buildings and staffing, which the education department often shares with the authority as a whole. Another form relates to level (primary, secondary, further) or interest (curriculum, equal opportunities). A third, common in county authorities, is geographical, with education offices serving different areas.

A fourth is the inspectorate or advisory service. The department is the servant of the authority – which is the members, acting corporately after advice from an education committee. The authority has a number of statutory duties and powers which it performs and exercises indirectly – through securing the provision and maintenance of institutions. (This indirectness will be increased if schools in its area opt for central rather than local maintenance.) The authority must see that its provision is efficient and sufficient. What this means is that the authority (the members) must be assured that provision is made and that the outcomes are acceptable. It needs an executive arm and a supervisory arm: or functional divisions and an inspectorate.

There might, for example, be four major executive divisions, concerned with teaching and other staff; finance and administration; sites, buildings and development and supplies and services. These divisions, or something like them, already exist in many authorities: their functions could be reviewed so that they encompass all the administrative activities of the authority. For example, the sites, buildings and development division should certainly be responsible for the reviews of provision which are currently undertaken as part of the responsibility of the officers for schools and further education. The nature of the finance division is already facing change in response to the generalisation of Local Financial Management. The staffing division could be concerned, not just with administrative questions of pay, conditions and contracts, but with the problems of the supply and quality of teachers over the authority as a whole.

The new executive divisions would make possible the elimination of that form of organisation based on levels or interest. Bringing those functions at present related to schools and other institutions within the divisions carrying executive responsibility would eliminate duplication and confusion and help to overcome a present perceived gap between policy and the provision of resources. It would also greatly simplify the administration.

A third form of current organisation, the geographical, is also brought into question when responsibility resides in institutions. In the experience of the Cambridgeshire pilot schools, contact with the area office has greatly diminished. Certainly a number of the allocative and control functions of the area education officers seemed to disappear. On the other hand, it is argued that the importance of area offices is not so much in the delivery of the service but in the reception of the public: people need an accessible place where they can get information and decisions. But the question then arises as to whether the area office is sufficiently local for this to be realistic.

Another Cambridgeshire innovation – of 'property bursars', based in large secondary schools and responsible for all the authority's property in the locality – suggests that the area offices are insufficiently local to be satisfactorily accessible. If they cease to perform an allocative and control function, there can be little ground for continuing their existence.

It would be consistent with decentralisation for the school to be the first point of contact for the public. Information, not only about the school itself, but also about other schools and council services, should be readily available in each school, and part of any departmental review would be directed to creating the conditions in which this could reasonably be the case.

The structure of the education department which emerges from these considerations is based upon two quite different functions. The first, executive, group is the responsibility of divisions responsible to a Deputy Chief Education Officer. The second, which is supervisory, is the responsibility of a non-executive inspectorate. There has been a clear gain in simplicity, rationality and comprehensibility.

There would be similar gains in the organisation of the sub-committees of the Education Committee. There would be four main sub-committees corresponding to the four executive divisions. (The inspectorate would report direct to the Education Committee, see below.) This would greatly enhance the capacity of members to hold officers accountable, on behalf of the public, for the way in which the authority performs its statutory functions. At present, members are tempted to concentrate on matters (such as the way schools operate) which they cannot and should not control and away from other things (like the efficiency of the office as a service to the schools) which they should.

There is one further point about the executive divisions and the officers who head them: it relates to the dual relationship they have with education and with the authority as a whole. For example, a typical Assistant Director, finance and administration (education), is responsible both to the Chief Education Officer and the Director of Finance. This dual accountability reflects an important fact about the local authority; it is a 'statutory person' – that is, it can do only what it is given specific powers to do by law. Broadly speaking, these powers relate to the provision of services, like education. The authority has no existence or function apart from the provision of these services.

In order to provide, it must put itself in a position to raise and distribute money, to manage staff and to provide buildings. The position of the ADFA(E) brings the authority's financial administration to the service of the education department and also controls the way in which the education department manages its finances. On the one hand the ADFA(E) is the Finance Director's accountant or bank manager; on the other he is the financial director of the Education Officer. He must see that education makes the best use of resources, but can help education to make the best use of the financial system. He remains respectful to good financial stewardship but looks for opportunities, in funding, for the Education Department: he can help education to get its share of available resources. This duality, of support and control, is inevitable and right, it is more effective than the pretentious wastefulness of 'corporate management'.

So much for what the local education authority provides, and the way it sets about this duty. What of the outcomes? An authority has the duty to secure that the education it provides is 'sufficient' and 'efficient'.

Specifically, 'secular instruction' in county schools is under the Authority's control – unless it provides otherwise in articles of government. The conduct and curriculum of schools, and their organisation, management and discipline, are a matter for the head and governors. (The government's current proposals will affect, but not abolish, these functions.) The instrument which the legislation provides to enable the authority to secure efficient and sufficient education and to exercise control over the instruction provided by schools, is the power, given in the Education Act 1944, S 77, to inspect the schools which it maintains.

The prime task of an inspectorate is to enable the authority to secure that the general standards of education offered are appropriate. They must inform the authority of how the system as a whole is performing. In a phrase used by HMI, an inspectorate acts as the 'eyes and ears' of the authority, seeking to satisfy it regarding the conduct and efficiency of all the educational institutions in its area. An inspectorate fulfils its responsibilities in three main ways: *assessment; advice;* and *innovation.*

Assessment is based on first-hand observation and intelligent enquiry in schools and other institutions. Inspectors have a responsibility to observe and assess any aspect of the life of a school or other institution which affects the educational experiences of the pupils or students. Following assessment, the inspector should draw attention to matters of importance and/or those requiring urgent action. In any school or institution, any such matter has first to be discussed with the head. Afterwards, the inspector reports to the chief inspector. Assessment includes recommendation of the confirmation of teachers on probation.

Advice is aimed at relieving difficulties or resolving problems already identified. Advice may be given to heads of schools and to other professional staff. It may also be given, as appropriate, on the educational aspects of the work of the education department. This advice may be sought or may be offered unasked. At all times advice has to be offered in such a way as to make it acceptable to those who are to take action on it.

Innovation should be justifiable in terms of the educational welfare of pupils and students. When good ideas emerge in schools, inspectors should recognise and support them and assist the schools to devise apt means of implementing them.

It is important to recognise that the inspectorate is not an executive division of the education department. Its job is assessment and advice – not action. The standing and acceptability of its assessment and advice depends upon a recognition of its disinterestedness. To put it baldly, if the inspectorate acts, who is to assess what it does? For the same reason, the inspectorate must be seen to be independent of the executive divisions. One of the things it may feel bound to report upon is the effect of executive action upon the educational experience of children in schools, either actual or potential.

There are weaknesses in the present character and organisation of inspection in many authorities. The division between primary and secondary is unhelpful, and makes it harder for the inspectorate to offer overall assessments of the working of the service as a whole. The primary inspectorate itself is of a character to enable it to fulfil its responsibilities in the schools. It is experienced in assessing the work of schools as a whole and in advising on professional matters generally. It is widely recognised that the secondary inspectorate, being a group of subject specialists, is less well placed. The general inspection of secondary education is not well served by the present arrangements. This is particularly important since studies of the effectiveness of schools seem to agree that specialist competence among teachers is not one of the most important things that go to make a good and successful school.

A further weakness concerns the amount of time which inspectors devote to activities other than inspecting. Individual inspectors differ, of course, and it is not easy to get any precise figures; but it is probably not unreasonable to assume that at present local inspectors generally spend only about one third of their time actually inspecting. The rest is devoted to matters of educational policy (attending committees and other meetings), curriculum development (more meetings and consultations), and in-service training (courses and conferences). This balance is unsatisfactory. It reduces, to too great an extent, the time spent on the inspector's chief task, which is to give the authority the means of knowing about the state of its education service.

In any reorganisation of an education department the place and function of the inspectorate is critical. The inspectorate should consist of a team of general inspectors, capable of carrying out their functions in any of the authority's establishments. Of course individual inspectors may have a subject or other specialism, but this should not be the prime ground for their appointment, and their task is a general and not a specialist one. An exception to this might be a senior inspector for special education – because of the statutory responsibility for this which the local authority bears.

The inspectorate should be headed by a chief inspector, appointed at an equivalent level to a deputy education officer. He or she should report directly to the CEO and to the education committee. It should be invariable practice that the CEO might not change any report from the chief inspector, though of course he might wish to comment upon it.

Each inspector should report directly to the chief inspector. There are no organisational grounds for intruding tiers of inspectors. For convenience, inspectors might be based in what are now area offices, or more localised places, but this need not affect the simple organisational principle. It has been argued that these local teams of inspectors need to have their work co-ordinated by a senior inspector. If this makes for convenience, it is acceptable – but not if individual inspectors are required to report through a senior inspector to the chief.

Policy

There remains the question of 'policy'. A reformed education department, as described above, would enable a local education authority to secure the provision of education and to be sure that it was efficient and sufficient, in other words to fulfil its statutory functions. But members and officers have got into the habit of thinking that they determine 'policy' and even 'implement' it.

Policy comes in many guises. Some of it is simply an expression of a function, as when an authority decides to gather all its 16 year olds in tertiary colleges – a matter for a development division. Another authority might have a 'policy' of protecting the curriculum as school rolls fall, which is a matter of making finance available above that implied by pupil numbers. Yet another authority might have a policy for enhancing provision for special needs in ordinary schools – but this again is a matter of provision.

But much local authority 'policy' is rather an attempt to do what is better done elsewhere. For example, a policy for science or French (over and above trying to recruit enough science or French teachers) is properly a matter for the schools. The school's responsibility will be undermined by the tedious vulgarities of the National Curriculum (until everyone loses interest in it, as they lost interest in the old elementary and secondary codes) but there will be no call for an authority to have a policy, except in the most general terms.

Other policies include equal opportunities and ethnic monitoring. Schools must, of course, obey the law in these matters: authorities that seek to do more are increasingly seen to be at best unwise and often merely tyrannical. Sometimes authorities are tempted to insist on particular management styles in schools. Such things are a matter for persuasion and influence, not policy – still less regulation.

The error here is in thinking that in education solutions are to be found in an office or a committee. Education is, on the contrary, a personal matter: it succeeds or fails with individuals, not with systems. The rational thing for an authority to do is not to say what policy is to be implemented, but what problems it believes to be important: it is for the schools to find the solutions. The authority may decide to apply additional money to help the schools, though this is seldom necessary or in the event effective. The authority learns about the effectiveness of the solutions from its inspectorate and can decide whether the problem persists or has been solved or superseded.

In short, Local Financial Management and other schemes of devolution will restore to members of local education authorities the important task of overseeing on behalf of the public the way the authority performs its proper functions. They need no longer be distracted by the temptation to know best how to do the jobs of others and, worse, to try to legislate their own prejudices.

Questions for discussion

1 *Would you describe the budgeting process within your LEA as 'integrated', 'historical', or 'independent', according to Tyrrell Burgess's definitions? To what extent do you think the budgeting process is understood by teachers and parents within your LEA?*

2 *Examine the four reasons given by Tyrrell Burgess for recommending the 'independent' method. Do they all seem equally valid?*

3 *Tyrrell Burgess argues for the simplest possible formula on the grounds that distribution on a more sophisticated formula, of the kind illustrated in Chapter 6 (see page 118), would be a serious limitation to real local decision-making. Do you agree with this point of view? If not, how would you seek to persuade your LEA to adopt a different solution?*

4 *Some LEA officers fear that the implementation of specific policy-based financial improvements will be undermined if the extra money is 'swallowed up' in a general formula. From what Tyrrell Burgess says in this chapter, how do you think these fears could be allayed? Do you agree with him?*

5 *Would you agree with Tyrrell Burgess's implicit assertion that the introduction of LFM implies structural reform of the LEA? Do you agree that this reform is necessary and to what extent do you accept the revised organisational pattern he proposes?*

6 *Tyrrell Burgess foresees the demise of the area education office in its present role. What problems, if any, do you envisage if all the functions of an area office were to be located in a designated school?*

7 *Are you able to provide examples of the 'pretentious wastefulness of corporate management'?*

8 *How acceptable do you find the idea that the inspectorate's role is 'assessment and advice, not action'?*

9 *If you accept Tyrrell Burgess's suggestion that the secondary inspector's task is general and not specialist, how might the specialist provision be made?*

10 *The overall thrust of Tyrrell Burgess's argument is that the LEA is to become an agent of oversight, persuasion and influence, while putting on schools the responsibility for finding the solutions. Do you agree with this and to what extent is it compatible with the Government's legislation in the 1988 Act?*

Chapter 8 Future perspectives

Brian Knight

In this concluding chapter, Brian Knight lifts our eyes from the short-term concern of devising financial systems that work to the more distant hills as he speculates on the possible developments that could be unleashed by LFM. His exciting, and at times controversial, ideas remind us very forcibly of what many contributors have stressed: money is only the means to an end. It is as educationists and not as financiers that we have to decide what our objectives are.

Local Financial Management is not just a shift in administration: it is, or will be, a school revolution. Its ramifications will extend far beyond mere finance areas of the educational system. This chapter is an attempt to foresee the changes that are likely to occur.

Some can be teased from the logic of the situation; others are much more speculative. For simplicity, I have used 'This will . . .' No arrogance is intended. It really means 'This may . . .' or 'This could . . .' (or perhaps 'This won't . . .').

The learning curve

Those involved with LFM will pass through stages, a little like riding a bike. At first one struggles just to stay on; then one becomes more adventurous; then one realises the limitations. During the first stage schools and LEAs will be mainly concerned with mastering the system and gaining confidence. This will probably take several years, because the cycle can only be experienced once in 12 months. Only training, and perhaps simulations, are likely to speed up the process. At first changes in a school's budget are likely to be pragmatic. There will be commonsense economies and adjustments, and relatively minor shifts of expenditure limited to a mere 2–3% of the total budget. These will still make a significant impact at the chalkface – sufficient to convince participants that the game is worth playing.

The second stage will be more thoughtful and analytical. It may begin with more systematic studies – perhaps an energy audit, a special study of school meals or the costs of the reprographics system, for example. A quest will begin for comparisons with similar schools, for otherwise how can a school judge its financial performance? There will be a growing, suspicious interest in the cost of central LEA services – because these will be seen as reducing the sum available for schools. Initially this is likely to be in services which can be costed and even recharged quite easily, such as an audio-visual service, school library service, central furniture store, etc. But in time sharp eyes will fall on the inspectorial/advisory service. Are we getting value for money? Perhaps even the administrative costs of the LEA, and the recharging from the authority's other departments will come under scrutiny.

At the same time, the approach to LFM will become more professional. There will be a better grasp of underlying concepts and even theory. The cost data will be re-examined and rearranged – prime costs versus subsidiary, fixed versus variable – because different views open new perspectives. And we may see an interest in subject costs, or even output costs, difficult and sensitive though these areas are.

The third stage will arise because this professionalism will inspire its own discontent. Once users of LFM reflect upon the system, they will realise its limitations. In most schools it will still be very difficult to make major shifts within the budget. Governors and heads will gradually see that their new freedom is largely illusory – that they have nothing like the freedom of their independent sector counterparts. They will realise that they are hemmed in with constraints. They are not master of the supply of funds, handed down by the LEA or central government. They may attempt to circumvent this by raising funds from other sources, but this is likely to be marginal for most schools. And they will certainly see that they are hemmed in by a host of regulations which severely limit their room for manoeuvre – on the school day, the school year, pupil attendance, the national curriculum, meals and free meals, transport, charges to parents. They will eventually see that financial delegation brings freedom – inside a straitjacket.

I have suggested elsewhere that 'a school is a cost-accountant's nightmare: a labour-intensive, non-profit-making service organisation, with ill-defined objectives, with uncosted and unquantifiable outputs and ill-costed inputs, in a straitjacket of constraints and with an arthritic lack of flexibility in buildings and staff.' It will be surprising if governors and heads, with their new-found financial expertise and confidence, do not eventually demand that the straitjacket is untied.

A more professional approach

Expertise

A by-product of LFM will be the growth of expertise in financial management. Heads and senior staff will acquire this, just as now they have acquired general management, pastoral care or personal relationships skills. Some will develop a special expertise, just as now some secondary heads are good timetablers. Governors, or some governors at least, will acquire it. LEA officers will need to have a comfortable knowledge of LFM, and area advisers rather more. And a more established role and career structure for bursars will emerge.

All this implies an explosion of training. Initially this will be troublesome, since the number of 'experts' available is very limited. Soon, though, good training materials and advisory support should be forthcoming. Eventually, qualifications in aspects of LFM may develop.

Statistics

Less obvious but perhaps more important will be the development of financial statistics. At present these are rudimentary, or worse. Few LEAs are capable as yet of producing a complete and accurate set of each school's costs.

Fewer still can provide useful unit costs, or comparative costs between peer group schools. And comparison between peer group schools of different LEAs, or matching against peer group averages for LEAs or nationally, is virtually impossible. Yet such statistics are essential for intelligent analysis, as the following example shows.

Take the electricity bill of £15 000 for The Mountaintop Comprehensive School (1000 pupils) for 1987/88.

What are we to make of this? Good? Puzzling? Extravagant? We need something to compare it with. Try uncovering the table below *one line at a time* (no cheating!):

Electricity, unit costs per 100 pupils:	1987/8	1986/7
1 Mountaintop Comprehensive School	£1500	£1400
What conclusions do you draw?		
2 Peer-group schools in the same LEA, average	£1520	£1470
What conclusions now?		

3 Peer-group schools, England & Wales, average £1400   £1350
   And now?

Line 1 You may feel that the increase of 7.1% is possibly reasonable, though it is higher than general inflation.

Line 2 Did you notice that
   i At Mountaintop, electricity costs less than in its sister schools?
   ii In the sister schools, the increase from 1986/7 has been less than half as much (3.4%)?

Line 3 I'm sure you saw that
   i The national increase (3.7%) was similar to the LEA schools, but . . .
   ii This LEA's electricity costs for this group of schools were higher than the national average.

Of course, questions may arise. Are the statistics sound and reliable? Is the peer group composition valid? Are there special factors? But without this sort of comparative information, the Mountaintop governors and head and the LEA officers can never begin to make sense of their financial information.

At present we are miles away from this. We do have the useful CIPFA national educational statistics. But they have serious shortcomings. The headings are not really designed for local use. They are not sufficiently disaggregated – for example examination expenses are submerged in 'other supplies and services' – and LEA compilation is still not sufficiently uniform. We shall need good national comparative data. Ideally the DES should require it from the outset. More likely we shall realise in about the year 2000 that it is necessary, and begin a painful process of statistics rationalisation.

In such a context, unit costs need careful treatment. 'Per 100 pupils' is often a good divisor – it gives one a better feel for the actual cost, and makes quick mental calculations easier. Other items need other units – hectares for grounds, meals for catering etc. And one needs to be alert to the washback effects. The Audit Commission supplies unit costs on services such as libraries by LEA families. These encourage LEAs to reduce above-average costs, but tempt departments to argue for increase if they are below the level for the family.

There needs to be discussion over what should be included in a standardised breakdown of a school's costs. At present meals, free meals, and INSET are costed separately in the CIPFA statistics. Logically they should be included, and probably they will be. Loan charges should in theory be included – though in practice they are not very meaningful, since they are recycled and it is difficult to establish what a school's actual debt charges are.

Certainly one might wish to include each school's apportioned share of LEA overheads. LEAs will resist this, on the grounds that it is a mere ledger transaction as schools can't control such overheads. However, this isn't quite true. As suggested earlier, once schools know what these overheads costs are, they will press to reduce them.

There will be one subtle and sometimes amusing consequence of LFM. That is, a tendency for schools to try to reduce their paper costs, either because this looks better in comparison with other schools, or because it enables them to make more favourable use of the formula allocation. So schools which now happily house a public branch library, or a youth club, or some other 'tenant', either free or for an unquestioned notional rent, will demand that a realistic rent be charged. This could have damaging effects for the community education sector, and is discussed further below.

Theory

Another professional development will be the growth of theory. Concepts of prime (ie 'chalkface') and subsidiary costs are scarcely used now. But establishing whether the proportion of subsidiary costs – meals, transport, aids to pupils, administration – is increasing (likely as rolls fall), or decreasing as primary enrolment recovers, will become increasingly relevant. In a falling roll situation, it will be important for a governing body to model, however simply, the growing pressure of fixed costs (premises costs, for example, are largely fixed.) This can be done by a simple formula:

Let C_1, C_2 = total costs at present, future point, etc.
Let R = percentage reduction in student numbers (eg 20, for 20%)
Let V = variable costs, as a percentage of total costs (eg 75, for 75%)

$$\text{Then } C_2 = \frac{C_1 \ (10{,}000\text{-}VR)}{10{,}000}$$

Example:
Let R = 25 (falling rolls %)
Let V = 80 (taking fixed costs, as say 20% of total),

$$\text{Then } C_2 = \frac{C_1 \ 10{,}000\text{--}2{,}000}{10{,}000} = \frac{C_1 \ 80}{100}$$

So, if a school's roll falls by 25%, with 20% fixed costs, its total costs will only fall by 20%. *If* its budget was reduced in line with its rolls, in real terms it would suffer a cut equivalent to 6.25% of its total reduced budget (and 7.8% on the variable part of that budget).

Such advance information enables governors and heads either to make allowance, or to agitate for an adjustment of allocation. Equally such formulas will be important for LEAs to adjust their allocations to schools.

Eventually, theories of financial management will emerge, comparable to theories in educational management, group dynamics, etc. We shouldn't be afraid of theory. LFM, whatever its practical guise, is already based on it, implicit or explicit.

Finally, we can expect growing professionalism to lead to the development of specialist publications and journals, conferences, and possibly even organisations. This has already occurred in the USA.

Delegation of supply

LFM is about delegation of responsibility for expenditure. At present there is no delegation of supply.

Increasingly heads and governors will chafe that the scope of their responsibilities – their power, if you like – is limited by the supply of funds. They will try to improve this for two reasons. First, they will be much more conscious of the value of switching, or augmenting, resources at the chalkface. Second, they will be much more confident in discussing school finances and better equipped to present a case.

Augmenting LEA supply can, and already does, take various forms. The most obvious is voluntary fund-raising of the traditional kind. Some schools are remarkably successful, and this is not just a simple index of their socio-economic context. So we may expect that given greater expertise, the greater prominence of the governing body, and greater parent participation, this aspect may expand. Such fund-raising will be particularly effective in primary schools, where the ratio of funds raised to capitation allowance tends to be higher. Equally likely to grow are the more sophisticated, covenant based 'enrichment' schemes originally pioneered by some Avon schools.

Another area likely to expand is industrial and commercial sponsorship. In recent years it has already grown rapidly with closer industry-education liaison and the impact of TVEI, and currently with the foundation of the City Technology Colleges. The most striking example is *Education 2000*, an innovative project piloted by a group of schools in Hertfordshire which receives extensive industrial backing. Again, LFM is likely to encourage schools to move into this field. And although the first heady stage of the TVEI gold rush is over, it is likely that schools will continue to tap funds from the MSC, DES Education Support Grants, and LEA central funds. We may in fact see some schools becoming entrepreneurial in nature, like some University departments.

Two other potential sources of funding are already well explored

– Joint Use schemes with local councils and community education developments. Some community colleges already have large budgets which receive considerable augmentation through their community links and activities. Community education has often created delegated budgets, and so it will fit well with LFM – but with the caveat referred to below.

There remains the vexed area of voluntary parental contributions. Parents already make these for voluntary activities like trips abroad, out-of-school activities, residential stays – and at home invest in computers, magazines, encyclopedias, music tuition and private coaching. Should – and will – LFM schools go further in tapping this market? After all, a school of 1000, with perhaps 800 families with an average disposable income of, say, £3000, has a possible market which it could tap of £2 500 000! Even 1% would bring in £25 000, an addition of 50% to the school's capitation allowance.

The hornets are now out of the nest. What price free further education? Equality of opportunity? What hope for the underprivileged? The thin end of a very large wedge? When do donations become charges? Lift up a donation and find a voucher? I will try to face some of these issues later. All I am suggesting now is that schools are likely to want greater control over their supply of funds as they gain independence through LFM.

Disasters?

Accidents

Murphy's Law will still operate. Somewhere among a hundred LEAs, a scheme will be badly thought out and badly administered – especially given the haste with which LFM is now being introduced. Even in Cambridgeshire and Solihull experience is still not very deep. And some LEAs do not have a good track record for financial administration. Some have resisted such simple changes as carrying over unspent balances at the year-end, or limited virement, so it will not be surprising if some of these make heavy weather of a much greater change.

Some schools too, will have problems. We already have some heads who aren't good at managing capitation, so for them the expansion doesn't look promising. Some governing bodies will be inept. And there will be more scope for malfeasance.

This kind of disaster will be the result of individual circumstances. But beneath it there are at least four forces which are likely to produce disasters somewhere in the future.

Formulas

Formulas are ultimately essential – no LFM scheme can rest for too long on historical costs – but they are also crucial and should carry a large health warning. First, experience in using them is still very shallow. Second, it is going to be very difficult to design formulas that cover the whole range of schools. Research evidence suggests that apparently similar schools can differ in costs far more than one would expect. The bulk of the peer group may be similar, but the extremes can range widely. Dr J R Hough (*A study of School Costs*, 1981) found in his studies in three LEAs that even when schools were divided into types such as grammar, secondary modern, comprehensive 11–16 and 11–18, in most groups the highest unit costs were 50% or more greater than the lowest. Other research suggests similar conclusions. Differences between similar schools in different LEAs are even more marked.

So if formulas are imposed insensitively and without careful research – and they will be – by LEAs, or even to some extent by the DES, some schools will become casualties, while others will revel in largesse. The problem will be compounded because initially some schools may not realise that they are being penalised and insidious damage will occur which will be difficult to correct. Of course in time formulas may fit better, though this may just mean that schools have grown used to an ill-fitting shoe.

Certain characteristics of formulas can be foreseen:

1 Simplicity will be preferred. LEA administrators prefer simple formulas because they are easier to operate and explain. There is a strong case for multi-factorial formulas – say with staffing in FTE rather than £s, premises elements based on detailed assessments of their running costs, and other elements related to pupil numbers, sometimes weighted. These would protect schools saddled with aged staffs or costly-to-run buildings. But the first implies mixing financial and non-financial units; the second, time-consuming surveys. So there will be a temptation to plump for simpler formulas.

2 Consolidation will occur. Formulas with various elements will tend in time to be simplified by consolidation into a global allocation. But this makes it harder to see how the formula has been arrived at, and how equitable the original elements now are. For example, it will be harder to see if the 'capitation' element is adequate if it is buried inside a global formula.

3 The average will rule. Formulas will tend to reflect the needs of the average. And since the majority of schools will be clustered around

the average, they will not be too sympathetic to schools which deviate from it.

4 Exceptions will be discouraged. Hard cases may be given special treatment, but it is likely that this will only be for a break-in period. There will be particular factors – split sites, socio-economic difficulties in the catchment area, ethnic minorities – but the tendency will be to play these down where possible, because of the complications and disparities they bring. Formulas are very public, so there will be less scope for the unseen helping hand.

5 Formulas tend to be static, because revision is troublesome and sensitive. But they get out of date quite quickly. For example, two 'identical twin' schools in an LEA would be equally affected by a given formula – but if the rolls or needs of one change more quickly than the other, the impact could be appreciably different within just a few years.

6 Formulas give a pseudo-scientific impression of certainty. But while they may automate annual decisions, they do not replace judgement. They actually highlight the need for it!

All this suggests that the development of good formulas is going to be tricky. In the long run they may well prove very effective, and probably better than the concealed, often unrealised disparities which exist now. But we do need to be aware of the dangers and of the essential need for good research, otherwise disasters will abound.

Cuts

If central government imposes cuts upon an LEA, it will be easier for it to cut LFM allocations across the board than to trim the various parts of the budget, as previously. Indeed, it may be suggested that this enables schools to select their own priorities (or as they will see it, choose their own poison.) It could lead to unsympathetic treatment, what the Audit Commission calls 'devolution of blame.'

Inflation

Inflation at present we do not take so seriously. But if LEAs do not make a realistic allowance, the effect on a school's budget is insidious because of the compound interest effect, for example:

If in 1990 inflation runs at 5%, and the Tightshire and Scroogeham LEAs only allow 4% and 3% respectively, the situation over the next five years is as follows:

	National 'School Costs Index'	Tightshire LEA Level of funding (4% incr.)	Shortfall in index points	Scoogeham LEA Level of funding (3% incr.)	Shortfall in index points
April 1990	100	100	—	100	—
1991	105	104	1.	103	2.
1992	110.3	108.2	2.1	106.1	4.2
1993	115.8	112.5	3.3	109.3	6.5
1994	121.6	117	4.6	112.6	9.0
1995	127.6	121.7	5.9	115.9	11.7

So, by April 1995 the real value of Tightshire schools' budgets has dropped by 5.9% (and the increase needed to right this in 1995 is 10.9% (5.9% + 5% inflation), while Scroogeham schools' budgets have dropped by 11.7%. Given the proportion of their budgets which are fixed or semi-fixed, the effect on the variable elements will be severe.

Falling rolls

There is little experience of severe falling rolls combined with LFM, but it doesn't look a happy combination. Fixed costs will increase disproportionately; any lag in staffing reductions could affect other parts of the budget; and LFM will probably reduce LEAs' power to plan strategically for falling rolls situations.

Community education

The omens are contradictory. On the one hand, Community Education fits well with LFM. It often operates like a small business, adjusting to market forces, maximising income and ploughing back profits. And it can be a powerful force in raising funds from the local community. It should gain from increased flexibility in the school budget. But it often operates in buildings which have not been designed for fuel economy. So some schools may clamp down on community use of premises, especially at those times in winter when they would otherwise be closed, or else attempt to levy an economic 'rent'. To make formulas adjust to expanding community use will be a difficult task.

The effect of LFM on the schools

Flexibility and autonomy

The most obvious effect is almost certain to be that schools become more flexible and autonomous institutions. Flexibility is usually regarded as a virtue for organisations, as it improves their ability to respond and adapt. So we should welcome it. However, it does depend on disasters *not* occurring. A school starved of delegated funds, or squeezed by inflation or its fixed costs in falling rolls, may have nil flexibility.

Autonomy we are more ambivalent about. It leads to local decision making and local priorities, but it also weakens central strategic planning. The contradiction is highlighted in 1987 by central government on the one hand delegating financial responsibility to schools, and on the other withdrawing their curricular responsibilities! It is doubtful if autonomy can be confined to finance, and much more likely that the new attitudes will spread to other areas of the school – including a demand from governors and heads for some restored curricular autonomy.

Diversification

Increased flexibility and autonomy will inevitably lead to greater diversity. There will be a tendency for schools to build up certain features – for example, science, or the arts, or community education – depending on their particular strengths and local needs. One can foresee schools developing a 'bias' for which they are known (as secondary modern schools were urged to do in the 1960s). This has already occurred in the independent sector, where some schools are known nationally for their swimming, or music, or technology. However, governors and heads will face investment dilemmas. Do they build up such 'features' at the expense of other areas or do they go for a less distinctive but all-round development? And what about weaker areas? Do they feed these, to build them up, or starve them, on the grounds that investment there will bring low returns (heads already face this dilemma in respect of allocating capitation.)

Flexibility will probably spread to staffing. In whatever way LFM allocation is made, it will allow schools to decide, within limits, what proportion they spend on teaching and non-teaching staffing. So some schools may opt more for teachers, others for equipment and facilities (although the room for manoeuvre will be less than at first appears). But could it ultimately lead to flexibility over teachers' contracts, given the problems that weak heads of departments, for example, will be seen to create? Significantly this flexibility already exists in the independent sector.

Diversification will probably be an improvement, an extension of the existing tendency for schools to build up areas of excellence. But there could, and no doubt will, be eccentric or unwise decisions taken by some schools. LFM will tend to magnify these, since it provides greater gearing for implementing a particular policy.

Divergence

Diversification is a form of 'horizontal' divergence. Schools will remain equal, but become more different. But 'vertical' divergence is another matter – schools will become less equal. Divergence will occur to some degree because of the arbitrary effects of formulas at the extremes, and because some schools are financially managed better or worse than average. However, this may not be too different from the existing divergence which is largely concealed, often unintended, but still quite substantial. But greater divergence may arise if schools take more responsibility for augmenting their supply of funds. Successful entrepreneurialism will depend on the abilities of a head, senior staff and governors; but it will be correlated with the socio-economic composition of the catchment area. It will be the schools of the plusher areas which are most likely to rise, and the inner city schools which are least likely. And the favoured schools will be doubly advantaged, because they already have a more amenable and advantaged pupil-entry and probably a higher reputation.

This divergence problem is haunting. It cannot be prevented by stopping schools raising additional funds. There is not a very strong argument for equality of misery. It can only be counteracted by the LEA identifying the disadvantaged schools and compensating them. This could be achieved through positive discrimination in formula allocation – and probably this should be done. But there are more subtle mechanisms than handouts. Matching grants are possible – matching, or more than matching, a school's fund-raising, to offset its disadvantaged position. Or grants could be awarded to such schools only if they met certain performance criteria (eg improved attendance, changes to courses). This development of compensatory LFM mechanisms, particularly to offset poor potential for local fund-raising, will be crucial in the long term.

Benefits

Finally, will schools gain from LFM?

So far omens are good. Pilot schools are enthusiastic. But this could be the halo effect of the innovation. The answer will lie in the balance of benefits over disbenefits, or vice versa. The most likely benefits are an increase in the total of real resources available, from greater efficiency, raising of additional funds, and pressure for cost- efficiency in LEA overheads; a closer matching of resources and locally perceived priorities; and greater financial flexibility and speed of response.

Possible disbenefits have already been reviewed: reduced real resources, given the operation of formulas, insufficient funds in a 'cuts' situation, and squeezed funds with inflation or falling rolls. To this can be added the 'distraction factor' – a new subsidiary activity to seduce or drive heads, staff and governors away from their prime responsibility of providing education.

The balance is impossible to forecast. Probably one's view is determined by one's position on the pessimist/optimist scale. It is possible to put up convincing gloom and doom scenarios, with schools languishing, under-resourced, underprotected, and overadministered. Personally I would take a different view. I see the Secretary of State busily sowing dragons' teeth everywhere – governing bodies from whom spring a myriad of warriors armed with the weapons of LFM to do battle with the forces of evil. Which politician or government could withstand them?

Effect on LEAs

LFM requires a change of role for LEAs. They will do less planning and directing. This could be a weakness. Economic rationalisation of premises and staffs as demography changes will be harder when schools are more autonomous. Policy making will be more difficult when schools decide whether they will allocate the funds necessary for its execution (unless LEAs develop mechanisms to earmark allocated funds for specific purposes.) It is difficult to see the justification for area offices when many of their allocating and approving functions are taken over by heads and governors, or superseded by administration by formula.

Other activities, however, will need to expand. Monitoring LFM will be crucial. If the LEA does not do it, who does? This will include improved technical monitoring – auditing – since there will be more scope for impropriety. But it will also need a structured evaluation programme to assess the efficiency of LFM in each school and its effect on the institution, people, and particularly on the quality of education. Since some LEAs are already weak at conventional evaluation of their schools, and since they know little yet about LFM, difficulties lie ahead. But effective evaluation must be a high priority.

There will also need to be expansion of advisory and support services. Schools will be working in isolation unless LEAs can advise both generally and technically, supply useful comparative statistics, support schools in circumstances of difficulty, and provide effective training. Area offices could possibly find a new role here.

Finally, as suggested earlier, LEAs will come under pressure to review and cost their own central services, and increasingly to charge schools for these. Since many of them are not very cost effective at present, this would be a welcome and long overdue improvement.

Perhaps LEAs should not be too gloomy about the future under LFM. After all, he who pays the piper . . .

Effects on people

Governors will initially be baffled and perhaps overawed by their new role. But some governors will have relevant experience. So specialisation within the governing body is likely to develop, possibly with a sub-committee. Soon governors will enjoy their new power, as too often in the past they have been groping for a role. But they will also be more vulnerable to criticism. In addition, managing a school's finances is going to take time. Governors will find themselves with the responsibilities of a local councillor, but without the kudos.

Heads are on the whole suspicious or apprehensive of the change. But the experience so far suggests that the skills required for LFM are not particularly complex – not in the same league as timetabling, for example. So most heads should learn quickly, and after a few years will be confident in the new role. But time will need to be set aside for it – not as much time as many heads think, but still time. So another pressure and responsibility will be added, at a time of new initiatives and other substantial changes. LFM does not look like a remedy for stress. Much will depend on the quality of the non-teaching staff responsible for the administration of LFM, and the ability of a deputy head to be responsible for it if this seems appropriate. Most secondary heads don't timetable, so a number will choose to delegate LFM.

Senior staff will increasingly become involved, as part of the senior management team, but also as individuals. Some will specialise in LFM, as some do now in timetabling. Others will see expertise in LFM as necessary for promotion.

Teachers will probably not become heavily involved unless they are specially interested or recruited to a sub-committee. Most of them will be too busy with their main commitments, and will see LFM as someone else's responsibility, again as they often view the timetable.

Non-teaching staff will often have increased responsibilities. The day to day administration of LFM depends on a reliable bursar or secretary. Many will become trained in IT.

The further future

At some stage in the future four new and inter-reacting trends will affect LFM. First, practitioners will become interested in costing not just inputs, but process and outcomes; second, they will become aware that all financial expenditure is converted into units of time-usage; third, they will then wish to throw off the constraints which restrict the exploitation of LFM; and fourth, the use of new technology will transform education and the financial system which feeds it.

First then, governors and heads will begin to look beyond financial inputs. After all, there is not *necessarily* any correlation between expenditure and educational outcomes. Spending more money on a particular area in a school does not necessarily lead to perceptible improvement. The first step will be to attempt to cost the process, perhaps by subjects and courses. Such costing is commonplace in the USA. Take Rhoda Dersh's comments for American parents, made a decade ago:

The Budget is your business for still another reason. It reflects the quality of management in the local schools. If the budget itself is disorganised and sloppy – if it is difficult for you to find the answers to such simple questions as 'How much did we spend last year on athletic programs?' 'How much will be spent for remedial reading this year?' – you can be pretty sure that the school management is disorganised and sloppy too. This certainly would suggest that money was being wasted, and also might suggest that education was suffering – if only because it is difficult for teachers and students to do their best in schools that are badly run.

Such 'simple questions' may not be too easy to answer. But eventually no doubt we may even see attempts to cost outcomes – subjects passed and grades attained.

It will all be a very frustrating business, because a school is a sealed system. Turning off expenditure in one branch will immediately be offset by increased expenditure in another. Suppose, for example, the governors of The Philistines Technical School decide to cut out Art and Music. Their pupils will still have to learn something in that time, requiring similar staffing, learning resources, premises and the same range of overheads. So the net saving is probably nil. Savings can be made by increasing class size of post-16 groups and eliminating small 11–16 groups, but those are often the only major savings possible.

So we shall then face up to the importance of the use of time for educational finance. We shall realise the obvious – that all expenditures in education buy physical resources which are then consumed in variable quantities of time usage.

Financial resources	→	*Physical resources*	→	*Time utilisation*	→	*The educational process*
(financial funds and capital resources)		People Premises Supplies and services Technology Catering and transport				

For example, if we invest in an expensive piece of new educational technology but it is only used for one hour per day, the effective input into education is only 10% of that when it is used for ten hours. Painfully obvious, but little understood. Our school financial systems are in bondage to our school calendars. 190 days a year, four hours forty minutes a day, is no way to run a key industry. And the quality of time is so poor. It is set in a rigid frame, ruled by seat-time where every pupil must warm his or her seat for the same quota of time. So attempts to address the *individual* needs of the learner are frustrated, the increasing capital investment in equipment in education is not cost-efficient, and the most cost-effective aspect of education (community education) is largely excluded from the main school day.

Eventually we shall realise that our current school day is a quaint relic from a potato-picking age. We shall design a day which provides flexibility for the learner, maximises use of new technology, and integrates the learning process for learners of all ages. A two part day is probably the answer – say 8.30 am to 1 pm, providing 75% of the curriculum conventionally, and 1 pm to 10 pm for the remainder, as required (and varying according to the learner's current needs), to make the fullest use of plant, equipment, learning resources, staff, and community volunteers for all who wish to train or learn from 5 to 95. Surely governors and heads will see – eventually – that such provision is a better and more flexible use of the financial resources they control?

At the same time, no doubt, they will question other constraints upon the effective financing of education: for example, the traditional school year, capriciously uneven and unpredictable for planning courses, and with the best unlearning device yet known to man beginning each July. Soon they will question other regulations from that earlier era – for school attendance, meals, transport, as well as the new regulations on the curriculum. They may even explore the possibility of marketing additional services to children and parents (as they already do to the community) for realistic charges. They will question all aspects of the status quo. LFM grants financial freedom – and in free air peasants lose their deference.

While this is going on, the landscape will be changing. The schools which governors and heads are managing today would be comfortably familiar to nineteenth century schoolmasters. They remain institutions with an industrial model of organisation but with pre-industrial technology. Chalk, paper and talk still rule. Only slate and spittle have been superseded. But we are now in the midst of that social, economic and technological turmoil, comparable to the Industrial Revolution, and variously called the Information Society, The Post-Industrial Revolution or the Third Wave. Its centre is the electronic storage, retrieval and transfer of information. And since education is largely about the transfer of information, and the ability to retrieve and learn from it, how long will it be before education is transformed, perhaps revolutionised, by the impact of new technology? How long before teaching spelling by hand seems as quaint and unproductive as handloom weaving?

When this change occurs, it will go hand in hand with LFM. LFM will assist, because it will be easier to switch expenditure from traditional to new learning systems. But it will be important for LEAs and central government to grasp what is happening and to supply the additional funds that will be necessary to prime it. And the radical changes in the system will solve many governors' and heads' preoccupations. They will improve the efficiency of learning; speed up the process; make cost comparisons possible between alternative systems (traditional teacher versus distance learning, for example); and make present constraints and regulations be seen as so absurd that they will be swept away.

Of course the future won't be quite as I have told it. But it won't be much like the present. I hope that as governors, heads and senior staff, bursars and secretaries, LEA officers and treasurers, parents and students struggle to master the intricacies of LFM, they will lift up their heads and take a longer view. LFM will be strange, often threatening, occasionally disastrous; but it offers us a freedom and flexibility in the state education system which we have never had before and which we desperately need. In the long run I sincerely believe it offers us a better future. 'What about me?' a child's voice pipes. Let us hope that we shall be able to offer him or her an education which is more efficient, more effective, more tailored to his or her individual needs . . . and no less humane.

Questions for discussion

1 *Do you think that the general educational changes foreseen by Brian Knight at the end of his article could be brought about* without *LFM? To what extent do you think LFM will assist or hinder these developments?*

2 *What problems can you foresee for the kind of flexi-time envisaged by Brian Knight on page 161. By what stages do you think such a process could be developed?*

3 *Compare Brian Knight's paragraphs on formula budgeting with those in Haydn Howard's chapter. To what extent have Brian Knight's theoretical fears been realised in the practical attempts to produce a formula in Cambridgeshire?*

4 *Compare Brian Knight's section on the effect of LFM on LEAs with that put forward by Tyrrell Burgess in Chapter 7. To what extent do they agree and disagree and which do you consider to the more probable as a course of future development?*

5 *Looking again at the closing visionary paragraphs of this chapter and bearing in mind John Brackenbury's phrase about the LEAs' inherent 'fear of change', do you think that Brian Knight's crystal-ball gazing will ever come about? What do you think the time-scale of such changes might be?*

Conclusion

This book appears to have dwelt in some detail on finance. I want therefore to conclude it by reaffirming that schools do not exist to provide examples of financial efficiency but to educate young people. Their prime concern should be to provide good teaching and learning opportunities in a caring and structured community.

The only reason for my personal interest in LFM and my commitment to it is that I believe that it enables a school to achieve these objectives more effectively than under the traditional arrangements for financing schools.

Through flexibility of response, speed of decision-making, incentive to make sensible savings, a head and teachers are freed from many bureaucractic hindrances and are enabled to carry out their task as educators more effectively.

The introduction of LFM in a school is an opportunity to ask some fundamental questions about the way a school is managed and invites us to reappraise our priorities. This may be a painful and unwelcome process but I believe it to be a necessary one.

It may well be that this book has raised as many questions in the reader's mind as it has provided answers. I would remind you that our purpose was not to offer a blueprint but to help you to short-circuit some of the possible difficulties so that you can make the most of the advantages that are on offer under LFM.

Lest the message appear to be a confused one, let me conclude by saying that, in spite of the reservations which have surfaced from time to time, I remain totally convinced that Local Financial Management is a most worthwhile development for schools and that, in the not-too-distant future, students of educational history will wonder why we took such a long time to adopt it!

Peter Downes

Bibliography

Books

A Study of School Costs, J.R. Hough, N.F.E.R. Nelson, 1981,
0 85633 163 5
Mainly concerned with national expenditure patterns and cost
comparisons between individual LEAs. Well documented with
statistical tables and has a full bibliography for those wishing
to make a serious study of the subject.

The Economics of Education, G.J.B. Atkinson, Hodder and
Stoughton, 1983, 0 340 33729 X
Useful for the historical aspects of educational expenditure and
for the relationship between national economic policy and
spending on education. Tackles some difficult issues such as
cost-benefit analysis and educational efficiency. Mainly of
interest to those who want an economist's perspective.

Managing School Finance, Brian Knight, Heinemann, 1983, 0 435
80480 4
Written from the point of view of the practitioner in school, this
book gives the newcomer to educational finance a thorough,
stimulating and practical introduction to the subject.

*Obtaining Better Value in Education: Aspects of Non-Teaching Costs
in Secondary Schools* Audit Commission, 1984, available from
HMSO
Looks specifically at maintenance and cleaning costs, but also
tackles delegation, recommending that local control of budgets
should be increased. Cautiously recommends that 25% of school
costs might eventually come under local control.

Towards Better Management of Secondary Education, Audit Commission, 1986, available from HSMO
Essential background reading for those embarking on LFM. Deals with school reorganisation to reduce waste, the delegation of responsibility to local level, allocation of teaching resources to schools, with a useful appendix on activity-led staffing.

School Budget: it's your money, it's your business, R. Dersh, 1979, National Committee for Citizens in Education, Suite 410, Wilde Lake Village, Columbia, Maryland, U.S.A.
The perspective from the United States where some versions of LFM have been in operation for a lot longer than in UK.

'School-centred financial management', *chapter by Audrey Stenner in Primary School Management in Action* (ed Ian Craig) Longman, 1987

Economics and the Management of Education, Falmer Press, 1987. See especially the chapter by Hywel Thomas on 'Efficiency and opportunity in school financial autonomy', which is particularly interesting in the way it shows how differently heads react to LFM.

The Promise of Self Management for schools: An International Perspective, Brian J. Caldwell, Institute of Economic Affairs, 2 Lord North Street, London SW1 3LB, 1987, 0 255362 93 5. A short survey of school self management in Australia, Canada, USA, England and Wales. Useful for international insights and broad conclusions.

Pamphlets and booklets

'Financial management in schools: the Cambridgeshire scheme 1982–83', Tyrrell Burgess *Working Papers on Institutions No. 53,* North East London Polytechnic, 1983.

Local Financial Management in Cambridgeshire, June 1986, National Union of Teachers, c/o R V Davies, 20, Kimberley Road, Cambridge CB4 1HH.

Local Financial Management: a personal view, P.J. Downes, November 1986, copies from Hinchingbrooke School, Huntingdon, PE18 6BN (50p).

Local Financial Management, Secondary Heads Association, July 1987.

LFM in a Primary School, Audrey Stenner, unpublished Ph.D thesis at the University of East Anglia.

Handbook for Financial Autonomy in Schools, published by Solihull Education Authority and available direct from them.

Open University Course E 325, see Block 5: School Resources.

Journal and Newspaper articles

'Making efficient use of scarce resources', Colin Humphrey and Hywell Thomas, *Education*, August 12th and 19th, 1983.
An explanation of the Solihull scheme at a fairly early stage.

Local financial management: a pilot scheme, Tom Hinds, B.E.M.A.S. Journal, Vol. 12, No. 1, Spring 1984
A useful summary of the Cambridgeshire scheme, written at a fairly early stage in its development.

Attitudes to Educational Finance, Brian A.A. Knight, B.E.M.A.S. Journal, Vol. 12, No. 1, Spring 1984
An amusing and provocative article, challenging educationalists to stop being coy about money and to come to terms with the real world.

'UK Research into School Costs and Resources', J.R. Hough and S.J. Warburton, *Economics of Education Review*, Vol. 5, No. 4, 1986, pp 383-394
Detailed research findings in four LEAs on substantial disparities in costs between apparently similar schools.

'Trusting schools with the money', Brent Davies, *Education*, 21 February, 1986
Explains the Cheshire scheme for secondary school controlled budgets and compares it with others.

'Local Financial Management, is on the move in Cambridgeshire', John Heywood, *Education*, 11 April 1986.
An outspokenly hostile view of LFM, particularly insofar as it will change the role of the Head.

'Delegating to schools' Colin Humphrey and Hywell Thomas, *Education*, 12th December 1986, pp 513-4
Useful summary of developments in Solihull so far.

'Dreams or nightmares?', Neil Fitton, *Times Educational Supplement*, November 7th, 1986

'Is devolution a delusion?', Bob Spooner, *Education*, 19 June, 1987.
    A clear presentation of the pitfalls of LFM, based on the writer's experience of a scheme in Leeds some 15 years ago.

'The power and the accountability', Philip Merridale, *Times Educational Supplement*, February 20th, 1987.
    The above three articles look at the likely impact on LEA powers and responsibilities if LFM is introduced across the country.

'Steering between two poles' Philip Merridale, *Times Educational Supplement*, August 14th, 1987

'Week by week', Jim Hendy, *Education*, 2 October, 1987.
    The Stockport Director of Education supports LFM but criticises the Cambridgeshire model.

'Control of the purse strings', Hilary Tagg, *Times Educational Supplement*, November 11th, 1986.
    A wide-ranging set of comments from Cambridgeshire heads after the decision was announced to extend the scheme to all secondary schools from April 1987.

'Not quite Grange Hill, plc', *The Economist*, January 31st, 1987.

'School Finance', Tim Simkins, *Management in Education*, Vol. 1, No. 2 Summer 1987
    Draws attention to the conflicting models of centralist and devolutionary policies in current government thinking.

'The Head was in his counting house' *Times Educational Supplement*, October 9th, 1987
    An account of the local financial management scheme in Solihull.

'Opting out will not mean opting in to financial stability' Tony Travers, *Guardian*, 8th December, 1987.
    Comparison of per pupil unit costs among LEAs, from CIPFA statistics.

Notes on the contributors

Peter Downes

After education at Manchester Grammar School and Cambridge, Peter Downes taught at Manchester Grammar School for 12 years, being Senior French Master for the last six. He became Head of Linguistic Studies at Banbury School in 1972 and was appointed Head of Henry Box School, Witney in 1975. After seven years there he became Head of Hinchingbrooke School, Huntingdon, a voluntary controlled comprehensive school of 1700 pupils and one of the pilot schools for the Cambridgeshire LFM scheme.

Peter Downes is a well-known author and editor of modern languages teaching materials, particularly *Le Français d'Aujourd'hui* and *French for Today* (Hodder and Stoughton). He has served as reviser and moderator for a number of examining boards and has assisted with several research projects in modern languages. For three years he was Chairman of the Joint Council of Language Associations' Conference. In 1986 the title of *Chevalier dans l'ordre des Palmes Académiques* was conferred on him by the French Government.

John Brackenbury

Educated at Dulwich College and Dartmouth, John Brackenbury served for 17 years in the Royal Navy. After a period in the youth service, he took a degree at Bristol University as a mature student. After a four-year spell as Lecturer at Loughborough College of Education, he became Warden of Impington Village College in Cambridgeshire, a post he held for 20 years. After retirement, John Brackenbury was elected as a district councillor and then as a county councillor (Liberal) from 1981–1987, including a year as Chairman of the Education Committee.

Robert James

Robert James was educated at the Leys School, Cambridge, and then joined the family construction firm as a surveyor on completion of his National Service. Apart from a period of recall to the army at the time of Suez, he has worked in the building industry all his life, and in 1985 became Managing Director of a group of construction companies. He has been a county councillor since 1964, representing Comberton. He has taken a particular interest in education and has served for many years on the schools sub-committee. From 1973–81 he was leader of the controlling Conservative group and has twice been Chairman of the County Council. He has had a close and continuing interest in LFM and is Chairman of the members' steering group for the scheme.

Audrey Stenner

Audrey Stenner read Classics at London University and was for nine years a teacher of Classics in secondary schools. After a maternity break, she returned to teaching – but in a primary school. She has been Head of Buckden Primary School for 12 years and has just completed her PhD at the University of East Anglia, taking 'LFM in a primary school' as her thesis topic. She has been a co-opted member of the Cambridgeshire Education Committee since 1981.

George Thomas

A history graduate of Birmingham University, George Thomas taught in two grammar schools before becoming a Deputy Head in a West Midlands high school. Since 1970 he has been Headmaster of St Peter's School in Huntingdon, an 11–18 coeducational comprehensive school of approximately 1400 pupils. He was one of the original six secondary school Heads who joined the Cambridgeshire pilot scheme in 1982. He has maintained his academic interests by being Chief Examiner for history with two CSE boards. He is also a JP and has recently been ordained priest in the Church of England.

David Hill

David Hill taught in London and Surrey before coming to a Cambridgeshire school as a mathematics teacher in 1964. He has remained in Cambridgeshire, teaching at two schools and at the Regional College, becoming Deputy Head in 1973. He was appointed Principal of the Sir Harry Smith Community School, Whittlesey, in 1975, leaving to become the Project Leader of the Cambridgeshire Local Financial Management Scheme in 1986. He attended the Henley General Management Course for Senior Managers of Industry on a ten-week educational scholarship in 1983. Since 1986 he has had the oversight of the implementation of the Cambridgeshire scheme into all 46 secondary schools and an extended group of primary schools. He has recently become involved in advising a number of local education authorities on the implementation of LFM.

Haydn Howard

After taking a degree in economics at Sheffield University and further training in chartered accountancy, Haydn Howard worked for Cumbria County Council as a group accountant. For eight years he was Assistant County Treasurer in charge of computer services. In 1985 he was appointed Assistant Director of Finance and Administration in Cambridgeshire, working specifically within the Education Department. Since 1987 he has been working freelance as a business consultant and as director of a computer business.

Tyrrell Burgess

Tyrrell Burgess is Professor in the Philosophy of Social Institutions at North East London Polytechnic. He has been external assessor to the Cambridgeshire scheme of Local Financial Management since its inception. He has been a consultant on educational administration to the World Bank and the United Nations Development Programme. He was also a member of the ILEA education committee. His books on education include: *Guide to English Schools; Education After School; Costs and Control in Further Education* (with Pratt and Travers); and *Records of Achievement at 16* (with Adams).

Brian Knight

Brian Knight was educated at Bancroft's School and Oxford where he read history. After teaching in the United States and Canada, as well as in Britain, he became Head of Holyrood School, Chard (in Somerset) in 1964. He has taken a particular interest in the relationship between finance and education and his book *Managing School Finance* (Heinemann) is widely recognised as essential reading for all interested in this topic. Since taking early retirement in 1985, Brian Knight has been a freelance educational consultant and is also an Honorary Research Fellow of Exeter University.